Stanley Lane-Poole

Sir Richard Church

Commander-in-chief of the Greeks in the War of Independence

Stanley Lane-Poole

Sir Richard Church

Commander-in-chief of the Greeks in the War of Independence

ISBN/EAN: 9783337115555

Printed in Europe, USA, Canada, Australia, Japan

Cover: Foto ©ninafisch / pixelio.de

More available books at **www.hansebooks.com**

SIR RICHARD CHURCH

C.B., G.C.H.

COMMANDER-IN-CHIEF OF THE GREEKS
IN THE WAR OF INDEPENDENCE

BY

STANLEY LANE-POOLE

AUTHOR OF 'THE LIFE OF VISCOUNT STRATFORD DE REDCLIFFE'

WITH TWO PLANS

LONDON
LONGMANS, GREEN, AND CO.
AND NEW YORK: 15 EAST 16th STREET
1890

ADVERTISEMENT

THIS SKETCH of the military adventures of General SIR RICHARD CHURCH is reprinted by permission from the *English Historical Review*. Its composition has been greatly assisted by the notes and suggestions of the Rev. C. M. CHURCH, who also placed at the writer's disposition a large number of unpublished letters and other documents illustrative of his uncle's career.

S. L.-P.

BALLAIGUES, VAUD:
August 1890.

CONTENTS

CHAPTER I.
THE EXPEDITION TO EGYPT, 1801 3

CHAPTER II.
THE ARMY IN SICILY, 1802–6 10

CHAPTER III.
THE DEFENCE OF CAPRI, 1806–8 17

CHAPTER IV.
THE IONIAN ISLANDS, 1809–14 24

CHAPTER V.
THE ARMY OF ITALY, 1813–16 31

CHAPTER VI.
THE BRIGANDS OF APULIA, 1817–20 38

CHAPTER VII.
THE WAR OF INDEPENDENCE, 1826–7 45

CHAPTER VIII.
THE CAMPAIGN IN WESTERN GREECE, 1827–9 59

SIR RICHARD CHURCH.

CHAPTER I.

THE EXPEDITION TO EGYPT.

1801.

THE War of Independence left Athens a heap of ruins: not the battered fragments of her imperishable art alone, but unsightly wrecks of modern houses, overthrown by Reshid's artillery. Even in the year of revolutions, the ominous epoch of 1848, when twenty years and more had passed since the surrender of the Acropolis, little had been done to repair the ravages of the war. Four streets of mean-looking houses crossed one another at right angles; above, on Constitution Place, rose the bald white outline of the palace; and miserable twisting lanes, with neither lighting nor pavement, bordered for the most part by wretched cabins or high garden walls, extended on either side of the main thoroughfares. One such lane, called 'the Street of Hadrian,' ran below the old wall at the north-east angle of the Acropolis, and in it stood a house familiar to every resident in Athens. It was built round an open court, in eastern fashion, with a cypress and a pepper-tree for shade and fragrance. One side was formed by a three-storied tower, a relic of the Turkish domination, still kept in a state of defence with a view to possible revolutions. On another side stairs led up to a gallery out of which three sitting-rooms opened. Beneath were the offices and dwellings of the trusty Palicari who formed the voluntary garrison of the house in all Greece least likely to need defence.

Its master was sure to be found, in the forenoon, in his corner of the divan in the reception-room, where a motley crowd of visitors was commonly assembled, smoking the long chibûk and speculating on the turns of politics—senators and deputies of the opposition,

Suliots of Albania, nomarchs of the islands, chiefs of western Greece attired in *floccata*, embroidered vest, and *fustanella*, save where the sense of fashion had prescribed the unsightly dress of the West. There sat Makrijanni, Monarchides, Argyropoulos, and Demozelio, the 'white devil' of Acarnania, his aides Mostras of Arta, Theagenes of Thebes—men who had given their all (such as it was) for their country. They were discussing the *immensi evenimenti*, the sequels of the Paris revolution of February 1848, the prospects of their friends in the Boulê and Gerousia, the raids of the brigand bands of Papacosta or Velenza, and all the news of the hour. The master talks freely, genially, humorously with his friends in French or Italian, and more seldom in Greek, his clear blue eyes flashing now and again as he denounces some treachery of the powers that be, or moistening with the warmth of enthusiasm as he recalls some golden deed; for age has not availed to quench the generous passion of his youth. His slight figure bears the stamp of the man of action, and his eager glance confirms it. All who surround him, Englishmen, Greeks, be they who they may, evidently revere him. For the master is Sir Richard Church, formerly commander-in-chief of the Hellenes in the war of independence, and still and for always the best-beloved Englishman in Greece.

In 1848 he was approaching his threescore years and five, and had sheathed his sword for many a long day. But few men had seen more service—more responsible and adventurous service—than Richard Church. His early commands went back to the days of the great French war; he had served under Abercromby and Stuart, Kempt and Hudson Lowe, and had met the armies of Ménou, Masséna, and Murat, in the days of the consulate and empire. He had seen the birth of the modern English army; and a handful of raw undermanned regiments had grown before his eyes into the victorious legions of Wellington. He had taken a foremost part in the long battle which England, and England alone, waged in the Mediterranean against the Napoleonic dream of eastern empire; Alexandria, Maida, Capri, Zante, Santa Maura, all these had viewed him at his post; and the man who landed at Aboukir in the opening year of the century, who had fired a salute in honour of Trafalgar, had conversed with *dolosissima* Caroline, queen of Sicily, and had passed through countless perils and faced a thousand ventures since then, lived to hear of France and Germany fighting on the Rhine. The soldier who fought against the first Napoleon, before he was emperor, survived to witness the fall of the Second Empire at Sedan.

It speaks well for the Society of Friends that so sturdy a fighter as Richard Church should have been born a quaker. He was the second son of Matthew Church, a merchant of Cork, and Anne Dearman, his wife, and was born in 1784. His school career was cut short by an adventure which was to be predicted in the son of such peaceable parents. Richard ran away, and took the king's shilling before he was sixteen. His father wisely abandoned the attempt to make a quaker of a son of war, and, instead of reproaching him, purchased a commission in the 13th (Somersetshire) light infantry. Richard was never a big man, but when he was gazetted ensign (3 July 1800) he was unusually small for his age, and apparently ill-prepared to battle with the hardships and privations of an eastern campaign.

Nevertheless to Egypt he went, when the 13th was despatched in the autumn of 1800 to join Major-General Cradock's brigade in the Mediterranean, on the most important service that England at that time had to demand of her little army. We find him in February 1801 on board the transport 'Adventure' in the harbour of Marmarice, on the Karamanian coast, where Sir Ralph Abercromby and Lord Keith had found refuge from the winter storms—rather, indeed, to their own surprise, for even their pilots were not aware of the existence of this opportune haven. The general, thus unexpectedly preserved from shipwreck, was busily collecting information, drilling his raw army, negotiating through Sir John Moore with our allies the Turks, and gathering horses and transports, with very disproportionate results; meanwhile the men were being practised in disembarking and landing under the imaginary guns of the enemy. From this scene of deferred expectation, Church wrote to his sister (10 Feb. 1801):—

We have been here about six weeks, but expect to leave it for our final destination in about a week more. It is the most *savage* country imaginable. You see nothing from the ship but the most tremendous mountains all round which form the harbour.

He was not favourably impressed with either the town of Marmarice or the people: the former was 'filthy,' and we quite believe it; 'the inhabitants are the most ferocious as well as the most indolent in the world'—a more questionable statement, since they once formed the best oarsmen in the Turkish galleys. Pashas then were much as they are now, but more splendid in dress, and at least equally addicted to coffee and pipes. Thunder-storms accompanied by heavy hail, and the nightly approach of wild beasts, added to the inconvenience of the camp, and even in February the heat and effluvia were distressing. The letter continues:—

> We are about two or three days from Alexandria, where the French have their chief army and where we expect the greatest resistance. It is reported that they have received a reinforcement of 1,800 men. . . . We have here *Le Tigre* and Sir Sydney Smith; he is to command a battalion of marines and seamen and act on shore:—with him there must be success. His dress is curious, a large pair of mustachios, a long blue cloak lined with ermine, gold epaulets, and a large sabre. . . .
>
> Shocking idea! five paras—a coin of this country worth only one halfpenny—is the inducement held out to these wretches, the Turks, for the head of a Frenchman, and wonderfully well it succeeds; but it matters not whether French or English, so they have an opportunity of murdering him; his head goes to the Grand Vizir, and the assassin receives his paras. The Greeks, who are slaves to the Turks and are Christians, are as opposite a people as possible, a brave, honest, open, generous people, continually making us presents of fruit. If they make any money by trade, when it pleases the Turk he takes it from him, and if he murmurs, death is his redresser. Oh, how I hate the Turks! . . .
>
> We, the army, certainly go through more than any people in fatigue, hardship, dreadful living, and storms: living on salt pork, towed three days astern of the ship, and still so full of salt you eat it with the greatest difficulty; foul water, maggotty biscuit: such living is common to us, and happened no less than four times riding at anchor, twice before enemy's towns—Vigo and Cadiz—and twice in Tetuan Bay. I felt that I never knew the real sweets of home, and how many dangers, hardships, and fatigues would I now go through, and smile at, for the happiness of a return home to my dear parents, sisters, and brothers.

General Abercromby sailed from Marmarice on 22 Feb. and anchored in Aboukir Bay on 2 March. For the third time Aboukir was to be the scene of a battle. Here Nelson had destroyed the French fleet in 1798, and here Buonaparte cut the Turkish army to pieces in 1799. The bay was now filled with English transports, bringing some 14,000 men to dislodge the French who defended the beach with all arms, including fifteen cannon on the sandhills. Stormy weather delayed the encounter, but on the 8th General Moore took his division ashore in open boats under the enemy's fire, and, forming on the beach, carried the French battery at a rush, seized four guns, and drove their two battalions from the field.

General Oakes with the other division repulsed the attack of cavalry and infantry, and sent the enemy flying over the sandhills with the loss of three guns. The whole position was brilliantly stormed, and the French took refuge within their lines at Alexandria.[2]

The 13th foot was not in the front at the landing, but it had its full share of work afterwards. Cradock's brigade, to which it belonged, formed part of the centre column in the advance of 13 March, and was exposed to a most destructive fire; and in the victorious battle of the 21st, when Abercromby fell, it held a critical position on the left of the British line resting on Lake Mareotis. It also took part in the capture of Rosetta and forced the surrender of Cairo, escorted the French army down to its embarkation in July, and witnessed the fall of Alexandria in August. Contemporary documents relating to the expedition are very scarce, and the following letter from Church to his mother (written, he says, upon 'the only sheet of paper in the camp') is therefore valuable.

Egypt, 7 Sept. 1801.

The two letters [not preserved] I wrote from Rosetta, my dear parents, must have long ere this arrived. We then were prepared to march to the siege of Alexandria, which was to be stormed on all sides, and would undoubtedly have been taken with a tremendous loss to both parties. Fate ordained it otherwise. General Ménou, having often tried the valour of the British troops in the field, and dreading the dreadful slaughter which would be made by the Turks on every armed as well as unarmed person (more particularly the latter), the evening [26 Aug.] previous to the assault sent into our camp his aide-de-camp with a flag of truce to ask for a cessation of arms for six-and-thirty hours, to consider the terms we had offered. Our commander-in-chief [General Sir John Hely Hutchinson] agreed to an armistice, in the course of which time General Ménou thought fit to capitulate, to the great joy of both French and English. Thus has the campaign in Egypt finished to the great glory of the British army. The 2nd of September 1801 was the memorable day when the grenadiers of the whole British army, under the command of Major-General Cradock, took possession of the heights and fortifications of Alexandria, and hoisted the British flag in place of that of the French Republic. The terms are the most honourable on our part. The French are allowed six pieces of cannon, six-pounders, and their private property, and small arms only; and without sacrificing one soldier we have possession of the whole of the transports which brought out the whole of Buonaparte's army, besides six new frigates (two sixty-four's), and a vast number of vessels of different sizes, upwards of 600

---

[2] See Sir H. Bunbury's *Passages in the Great War*, pp. 93 ff.

pieces of ordnance, principally brass, besides thousands of all descriptions of stores, and granaries full of wheat and rice.

The taking of Rosetta, Aboukir, Cairo, and Alexandria, with a number of small forts and castles all through the country, afforded us a vast deal of trouble, and is expected to yield us some prize money. We landed in this country 14,000 men to attack 22,000 French bayonets (from the French returns for embarkation), and before the arrival of any troops from Europe three battles were fought between us, in every one of which we were victorious. The landing on 8 March gave us a footing in the country; the action of the 13th insured that footing to us by driving that enemy from the heights they occupied, and the glorious battle of the 21st sealed, with the death of our noble commander-in-chief, the entire possession of the country to our arms. Ménou shut himself up in Alexandria, and Belliard retreated to Cairo in the greatest precipitation. We followed up the blow, leaving a sufficient force to guard the heights in front of Alexandria. The remainder of the army marched for Cairo, and on their march reduced Fort Julian, a strong fort at the mouth of the Nile, took Rosetta and a fort on the bank, and encamped before Gizeh, a town at the opposite side of the river from Cairo. We were hardly arrived ere the French sent in an offer to surrender on the terms which they should propose. With some alterations we agreed to them; their private property and some pieces of ordnance were no object to us. Our numbers at the greatest calculation amounted to about 5,000, and theirs at the smallest were 9,500 fighting men. A few days were allowed them to get ready; they marched to Rosetta to embark, French in one column, English in another, and they embarked at Aboukir to the amount of 20,000 persons of every description.

Once the French under General Belliard embarked, the general lost no time. We proceeded to Alexandria and invested it on all sides. General Coote with a division of the army landed to the westward; we on the eastward made a false attack, which deceived the enemy; they turned their attention to us; in the meantime General Coote surprised the castle of Marabout and landed his army to the westward without the loss of a man. On our side we were equally fortunate. It was the dead of the night, and so dark that we got, without being perceived, within the range of the guns on the batteries; the guns had no effect, their whole line appeared one blaze and one continued roar of thunder, all to no purpose; we gained our own line with the trifling loss of a few horses. The next night we cut off the whole of their picquets, took seven officers and a hundred and twenty men; our loss was trifling. Our works to the eastward approached every day; from our trenches we picked their artillerymen from the guns, our *friends* the Turks were excellent at *that*: they would lie the whole day behind anything that would conceal them, purposely to pick off the men on the front lines or any other situation. They are the greatest cowards in the world; they never once fought with us in the field. At last our force on their right, the sea to their left, an army in front, and an army in their rear, cut off every chance of supply; we harassed them day and night. The 'heroes of Italy' were obliged to surrender to the paid troops they despised so much on hearing of their arrival in Aboukir Bay. . . .

Impressions of Egypt—'this infamous country'—follow, such as might be expected from a young ensign with little opportunity for close observation. He has seen 'everything worth seeing—the Pyramids, Pompey's Pillar, Sphinx, Cairo, Rosetta, and Alexandria, the Delta, and the country all along the banks of the Nile;' he has encountered 'reptiles of all sorts, a dreadful scorching sun, deserts without a drop of water,' and sums up Egypt as a country with 'some good qualities, though but very few.' The principal amusement of the inhabitants appeared to be smoking, and though there were Christians at Rosetta, it was hard to distinguish between them and the Turks, when it came to cheating. Like all Englishmen, Church admired the Mamlûks, but even at this early period the Turks excited his utmost scorn and detestation.

We had at Cairo the Grand Vizir and his army. We have here the Captain Pacha and his also—such a set of villains never were seen before; they go loaded with arms to molest every one they meet, yet are the greatest cowards in the world. The greater the rank the greater the rascal! From seven months' residence in the country I know so much of the Arabic language as to be able to converse with the Arabs; the French speak it fluently. I must now conclude about Egypt, only add, once out of it I would never wish to see it again.

A soldier could hardly begin his career better than in the Egyptian expedition of 1801. It was commanded by officers of exceptional ability and character, and its success effected a signal change in the position of the English army. Before 1801 we were discredited, and it was believed, not only abroad but at home, that our officers could never cope with Buonaparte's 'heroes of Italy' and of Germany. Alexandria restored our confidence, and England began to recover her faith in her generals. Richard Church shared in this revival of hope, and it was his good fortune to bear a hand also in the next triumph of the British arms: Alexandria and Maida were the prelude to Talavera, Vittoria, and Waterloo.

CHAPTER II.

THE ARMY IN SICILY.

1802-1806.

THE illusive peace of Amiens in 1802 interposed a brief truce in the war between England and France, but in 1804 Richard Church shared in the patriotic fervour which lined our southern coast with hundreds of thousands of troops, militia, and volunteers, eager to repel the invasion of 'the common enemy of Europe.' Buonaparte's vast preparations for the conquest of London, his thousand transports at Boulogne, and the splendid troops which were massed on shore ready for instant embarkation, had roused England to strenuous exertions, and recruits and reserves mustered so rapidly that the regular infantry, which in 1803 was reckoned at 40,000 (and this figure exaggerated the effective strength of the thinned and worn-out battalions) sprang at a leap in 1804 to 75,000, besides 80,000 militia and no less than 343,000 volunteers. Never had the nation more heartily responded to the call of the crown. To present anything like a practical opposition to Buonaparte's veterans, however, these large bodies of raw recruits and volunteers needed constant drilling ; camps of instruction were forthwith established along the Essex, Kentish, and Sussex coasts, and Sir John Moore at Hythe set that model of discipline which, emulated by the other camps, served more than anything else to prepare our soldiers for the long trials and triumphs of the Peninsular campaign.

In one of these camps at Hailsham—'a paltry place, but still on the coast (sic), and an advanced post, which is the only satisfaction we have to enable us to bear it '—Church and his new regiment, the 39th, into which he had exchanged, were stationed, and here he had the time and opportunity of learning those lessons in the art of war which the brief campaign in Egypt could scarcely have taught him. But he was not long forced to endure the rustic monotony of Hailsham, lighted up, as it was from time to time, by rumours of the approach of that hated enemy whose ships lay almost in sight across the narrow strait. The 39th were on their way to the Mediterranean in the spring of 1805, though what they were going for they knew not. That they were going to fight 'Bony' somewhere was enough.

Few people take much interest in the minor efforts of the great French war; yet they sometimes presented features of romance and opportunities for daring and resource such as the movements of great armies rarely afford. Nor were they without their due effect upon the main struggle. The unremitting attacks of our small forces in the Mediterranean upon every possible vantage-ground of the enemy drew off large detachments of the French armies from more vital spots, and, while depriving Buonaparte of many important depôts for arms and supplies, effected what was at least equally important, by raising the credit of the British army wherever it landed, and showing Europe that, if we could not turn out vast numbers of troops, at least those who did battle for us knew how to fight. The dash and vigour of our onslaughts upon the French positions in the Mediterranean, from Alexandria to the islands of the Adriatic and the bay of Naples, did much to restore that prestige which the triumphant course of French successes had impaired.

The expedition with which Church sailed, on 19 April 1805, consisted of about 7,000 men under the command of Sir James Gibson Craig, who was to proceed to Malta and thence carry on operations, of what description the government had no precise idea, except that they would be against the French in Italy or Sicily, or perhaps Sardinia or Minorca, according as circumstances and instructions should dictate. The principal object, however, was to keep the treacherous court of Naples out of the arms of the French, and for this purpose to land in Italy, in company with a large force of Russians, then at Corfu, and to endeavour jointly to protect the Neapolitan capital from invasion. It was a curious plan, and with such allies was bound to fail; but at least it did not lack able officers. Craig, Sir John Stuart, Fox, and Sir John Moore successively held the chief command in Sicily, and they were admirably seconded by men who afterwards made their mark in greater fields, such as Lowry Cole, Hudson Lowe, Ross of Bladensburg, Kempt, and Sir Henry Bunbury, who has ably recorded his recollections of the military operations of the time.

The expedition did not reach Malta till July. Alarms of the French fleet and a long detention at Gibraltar, where it had to wait for further orders, delayed it ; but to one at least of the officers the interval of leisure was not unwelcome. Church was for his age an ardent student, and took a keen delight in French and still more in Italian literature. At Gibraltar, when there was no Spanish gunboat to be attacked or avoided, he spent his time 'reading the few books I have, amusing myself with fortification, as usual, occasionally taking a row about the fleet, bathing. Ossian, Ariosto, and Plutarch's Lives are my chief authors, and one constantly relieves the other.' He was very romantic, and his letters are full of poetical quotations, varied by metrical outbursts of his own.

At Malta the young lieutenant of the 39th received unexpected promotion. He was made adjutant of the light battalion then being formed under Colonel Kempt. Writing from Valetta, 5 Oct., he says :—

The several light companies (Chasseurs) are embodied and made for the time being one regiment, to act, when in service, as sharpshooters, riflemen, &c., and to form invariably the advanced guard of the army. We consist of 890 select men, from all the British regiments on the island, and placed under the command of Colonel Kempt, a very excellent officer, who was military secretary to Sir R. Abercromby in Egypt and in all his campaigns elsewhere. I am placed on the staff as adjutant to the light infantry battalion. Believe me that I am sensible that there are many officers whose abilities make them more fit for the situation. There were no less than fifteen applications made by different officers, and all strongly recommended by their commanding officers, and I am really astonished to find that I succeeded in obtaining what I so little deserved or expected. It is of all others the most advantageous situation an officer of my rank could obtain, and to me the most flattering. You know that I am devoted to the life of a soldier and can relish no other, so I have at least that to urge in my favour ; inclination will not be wanting in doing my duty, whatever may be the case with the abilities. I have at last stepped out of the common track in the army, and I sincerely hope never to return into it again.—We sail to-day [he adds, 8 Nov.], supposed for Naples, and it is believed we shall proceed 200 or 300 miles in Italy without having any affair with the French. A great many regiments who served in Egypt are with us, and if we meet the ' invincible army of Italy,' I hope grenadiers and light infantry of the British will be able to give a good account of them.—The last cannon from the fleet has fired.

It was a fine sight to view the flotilla of more than a hundred ships making out of Malta harbour, and finer still when nine Russian ships of the line and eighty-five transports joined them off Syracuse; and the fact that all this brave array was bound on a bootless errand did not at the moment diminish its imposing effect. Ten days they tacked in sight of Etna, and at last weathering the western point of Sicily—for the fleet was too large to risk the passage of Scylla and Charybdis,—they began to disembark at Castelamare on 20 November. Here Church's duties as adjutant began in earnest, though indeed the beginning seemed more like play. There was a grand review of the troops before the king of Naples, and exultant volleys were fired by the British when at length the tidings reached them of Trafalgar and 'the glorious 21st of October.' Then up the country they all marched, and occupied the defiles of Itri and Fondi, and other strong positions. They little knew then what was going on beyond the distant Alps, but the disastrous news travelled fast. Mack had capitulated at Ulm; the fatal field of Austerlitz had been fought and lost; the French were advancing in overwhelming force upon Naples; and the perfidious court of Ferdinand had already submitted to the demands of Buonaparte. There was nothing for it but to beat as dignified a retreat as circumstances permitted. General Craig on his own responsibility, and in spite of the remonstrances of our minister, Mr. Hugh Elliot, re-embarked his army on 20 Jan. 1806, and set sail for Messina.[3] He was only just in time. What happened in the next three weeks may be told in the words of the contemporary Neapolitan historian Coletta :—

The king, queen, and the royal family flying, the Princes Leopold and Francis retreating with the army through the Calabrias, a timid and inexperienced regency in Naples, the kingdom laid open to hostile armies, the city undefended, the partisans of the king fugitives or hiding, the mob fluctuating between lust of plunder and fear of chastisement, the honest with arms in their hands for the defence of their own lines and for the maintenance of order in the city :—such was the state of Naples in the first days of February 1806, while at the same time 50,000 French under Marshal Masséna were conducting to his throne Joseph Buonaparte, with the name of lieutenant of the Emperor Napoleon.[4]

Sicily now assumed a double importance in the eyes of England. It was her advanced outpost against the enemy, and must be held at any cost against the army which General Regnier was leading into Calabria with the express design of reducing the remnant of

---

[3] See Mr. Oscar Browning's article on 'Hugh Elliot at Naples,' in the *English Historical Review*, No. 14, April 1889.

[4] *Storia di Napoli*, ii. 10.

the Bourbon kingdom, which Buonaparte had declared to be extinct. The Neapolitan court, piqued at our retreat, had at first forbidden a single English soldier to land at Messina; but no sooner had the queen taken refuge at Palermo than fear got the better of resentment, and General Craig was invited to disembark his troops for the protection of Sicily. It was a welcome bidding, for four weeks in transports had not improved the health or temper of the men. The English army, numbering about 7,500, was now posted with its centre at Messina, the left fortified at Milazzo, and the right stretching towards Taormina and Cape Passaro. An active flotilla of Sicilian boats scoured the straits, and a corp of natives was raised in our service. Church was zealous in his duties as adjutant of the light division; he was at the taking of the fort of Scylla, which guarded the straits on the opposite shore; and his familiarity with Italian brought him into useful intercourse with the Sicilians, among whom he mentions ' about 1,000 friars and monks, the apothecaries and parsons in the six parishes around our cantonments, many of whose names I do not know, and all the fishermen from Messina to Scarletta, whose names I *do* know, because I have them registered.'

He was already beginning to exercise that influence over foreign peoples which afterwards became the chief pride and delight of his life. In the same letter he records his first experiences of an earthquake, and its different effects upon the English soldiers and the Sicilians:—

A battle is nothing to it; it was a most deplorable scene to see the whole of the inhabitants on their knees, in the middle of the street, in the most dreadful rain. The villagers were surprised and enraged to see us performing all the duties of the regiment as if nothing had happened, and in a great degree they attribute this event to our being in the country.

The daily sight of the French encampments across the narrow straits irritated our men beyond measure, and in the summer plans were matured for anticipating the threatened French invasion by a landing upon the Calabrian coast. Church had gained credit by the zeal of his service, and in the arrangements for the advance he was attached as brigade major to Colonel Kempt's division.

His zeal and attachment to the duties of his profession [wrote Sir J. Stuart, the hero of Maida, to the Horse Guards] were conspicuous in a series of services that occurred within my own observations. I hardly know a more promising young man, or professionally a more deserving one. I gave him to Kempt as brigade major at Maida, and he always fully appreciated him.

The battle of Maida is the best known of the military operations during the occupation of Sicily.[5] It was in effect a successful sortie of the British garrison against the advanced position of the French army on the Calabrian coast. The English to the number of 5,000 landed on 1 July in the bay of St. Eufemia; the battle was fought on the 4th. The marshy plain of the river Lamato, which lay between the forest of St. Eufemia and the hill of Maida, where the French were posted, formed a most unhealthy camping-ground, and had the French left us alone the battle might never have been won.

The English army, massed on the heated sands of that desert beach, struck during the day by the burning rays of the July sun, and by night breathing in the pestilential vapours of the neighbouring marshes, were sickening and on the point of abandoning the enterprise, when Regnier, longing for revenge, flung himself upon their camp; he who had fought unsuccessfully against Stuart in Egypt hoped a return of fortunes in Calabria.[6]

In vain: he was completely routed; Kempt's light brigade broke the attack, and pushed the enemy relentlessly over the plain to the slopes of Maida; the guns and stores collected for the invasion of Sicily fell into our hands; Lower Calabria was cleared for a time of the French; the victory broke their prestige, and raised the spirits of our army. The pity was that it was not followed up.

In August of the same year, Church was entrusted with a mission which called forth to the full those qualities which afterwards proved so valuable against the secret societies of Apulia. At this time the Sicilian authorities, aided by Sir Sydney Smith, were encouraging by every means in their power the numerous bands of *masse*, or banditti, which the barbarities of the French army had fostered among the miserable population of Calabria. No weapon against the enemy could be neglected, and war, as well as adversity, sometimes makes strange bedfellows. To investigate the doings of these disreputable allies, and to discover the strength and position of the French troops, became a matter of necessity; and the task demanded not only considerable courage and presence of mind, but

---

[5] The best account of this and other military operations in the Mediterranean during the great French war is to be found in Sir H. Bunbury's *Passages*.

[6] Coletta, vi. 14.

a familiarity with Italian. Church was in a manner marked out for the work, and he hastened to volunteer. The risk was so great that his colonel, the Hon. Lowry Cole, hesitated for a whole day and, even when he had consented, knew no peace of mind till he saw the young officer safe back again. Accompanied by only twelve Neapolitan cavalry, Church pushed his reconnaissance to Nicastro, where he found matters in a critical state. The brigands were pouring into the town to the number of 1,500, murdering the inhabitants in the streets and making targets of the syndic and other notables. It was then that Church displayed that cool mastery over lawless ruffians which so often, in after years, stood him in good stead. With his twelve men he not only drove the *masse* out of a house which they had attacked, but ordered the chiefs to leave the town, an order which, strange to say, was for the most part obeyed. All night, however, his little company had to patrol the streets, and it was not till morning that he felt he could safely leave Nicastro, restored by his efforts to comparative tranquillity.

For this service, and for his detailed report on the movements and positions of the French, he received the thanks of Generals Stuart and Fox, and was shortly promoted to the rank of captain in the Corsican Rangers. But the chief reward to one of his chivalrous nature was the thought of the rescue of hundreds of women and children from the tender mercies of the brigands. He had resolved to 'perish rather than leave the helpless people in the hands of assassins,' and a sentence in a letter to his mother shows us the generous humanity which was ever his characteristic :—

> I feel more real pleasure at having been the sole instrument in the salvation of these hundreds than in having assisted in the destruction of the thousands of our abominable and treacherous enemies at Maida.

CHAPTER III.

THE DEFENCE OF CAPRI.

1806-1808.

A MONTH before the battle of Maida, Church had written home (10 June 1806), 'Sir S. Smith sails this day. On his way here from Gaeta he took the island of Capri in the bay of Naples. Colonel Lowe with five companies of the Royal Corsican Chasseurs sailed four days ago to garrison the island, as an attack from the French is daily expected.' Capri now formed a sort of vedette of the Sicilian garrison, whence a sharp look-out could be kept upon the enemy's doings in Naples, and communications established between the English army and the continent. It was a post for bold and venturesome men, and the authorities instinctively sent Church to the point of danger as captain of the Corsican rangers. For two years, from October 1806 to September 1808, he commanded the upper town of Ana Capri, which looks down eastward from its lofty terrace of lava over rugged precipices to the Marina and Lower Capri, and on the west hangs steeply over the blue waters of the Mediterranean. Colonel Hudson Lowe in the nether town placed entire confidence in his lieutenant above; and, unlike some others, Church always entertained a warm esteem and affection for his commanding officer, who, whatever his faults, was at least a gallant soldier.

At first the novelty of the situation, and the delight of flaunting the flag of England in the very eyes of Joseph Buonaparte over the way at Naples, were pleasurable enough, but after a while the monotony of the place and the association with none but foreigners began to weary him. He describes his life in a series of letters to his sister :—

14 Oct. 1806.

How fast is the scene changed! A twelvemonth has not yet passed and I have written you from Malta, from various parts of Italy, from

Sicily, from Calabria, from Sicily again, from Capri. I have been repeatedly changed on duty from one of these places to another; served an unsuccessful campaign allied with the Russians against the French in Italy; and been on a most glorious expedition against the same enemy in Calabria. I have been under arms three times to be reviewed by two crowned heads—twice for the king of Naples, once for the king of Sardinia. I have witnessed an earthquake; scarcely been, even for a week, out of sight of Mount Etna, Vesuvius, or Stromboli. I formed a party with the army selected to besiege Scylla, and was at the taking of it; and have had the *good luck* to have been *actually* shipwrecked at Charybdis; and have been no less than seven times embarked, and as often landed, . . . mixed up alternately with Russian and Neapolitan troops, Calabrese, Sicilians, and French. . . . I have served in the various capacities of lieutenant, adjutant, brigade-major, and captain, and have had no less than four different commanding officers in that space of time. To conclude this history, I am now, through the great favour of my present commanding officer, Colonel Lowe, duly installed captain-commandant of Ana Capri. . . .

From Capri you have the most beautiful view imaginable of Naples and Vesuvius, as well as of Baiae, Pozzuoli, the Elysian fields, Portici, the palace of La Favorita, and all the towns in the bay of Naples towards Castellamare, . . . the islands of Ischia and Procida, and Ponza in the bay of Gaeta, and on a very fine day, with a glass, Gaeta itself. You have a fine view of the Apennines and the highlands in the Neapolitan territory for many miles. From the back of the island you command a prospect of the gulf of Salerno and the various towns on its shores. So much for the views: now for the island itself. It is about $5\frac{1}{2}$ [$3\frac{1}{2}$] miles in length, and perhaps its greatest breadth is not above two. It is divided in two parts, Capri and Ana Capri, and has three towns, or rather villages, several convents, and a bishop, and several remarkable ruins of palaces, &c., built by Tiberius when that wretch made the island his place of residence. The whole island is a perfect garden, is covered with vines, figs, &c. Capri is the chief town and port, and has a castle; it is the seat of government and headquarters of the regiment, and has about 3,000 inhabitants; the roads are all very hilly, narrow, and, for the most part, *in steps*. Ana Capri is above two-thirds of the island, and once up, a level terrace abounding in fruit, wine, and oil; it has no place of anchorage for shipping, but several creeks and small bays where an enemy may attempt a landing. The only road from Capri here is (do not be surprised at an absolute fact) up a rock, cut into 600 [535] perpendicular steps, and this is the only communication between the two places. . . . Fancy my leading a high-spirited Arabian horse up these steps, which I have done, and he is the only horse in this part of the island. . . . My residence is in the Palazzo, a delightful house, one of those belonging to the many Neapolitan nobility who formerly spent a month or two of each year here previous to the French occupation.

I am sole governor here, civil and military; my military force consists of two companies, besides an officer's detachment of forty men, making my regular troops about 200, and two four-pounders. Besides these I have about sixty militia, and some few of the king of Naples' gamekeepers. I am at the advance post, the first to be attacked when King Giuseppe shall be that way inclined. I am totally independent of the commanding officer, except what relates to the regiment, and communicate with him by telegraphic and night signals. The population consists of about 900 people, not one of whom can go down to Capri without my passport. There is here a convent of nuns and a college for ecclesiastical education. I am on great terms with the *abbadessa*, a most respectable old lady, who was obliged to fly from Naples by the French, and is much attached to the English. We correspond almost daily, and as often as possible I make her a present of fish, fresh butter, hams, and anything else that I accidentally pick up. . . .

On 3 Nov. 1806 Church writes to his mother:—

My time is at present occupied in entrenching this part of the island, making a harbour, building towers of defence, making roads—anything whatsoever that renders my post so strong as to be able with a very few men to defend the place against whatever number of men *King* Joseph may think proper to attack me with. . . . These works, and exercising the men, signing passes from this to Capri for the country people, and now and then a ride or walk round my whole territory, or a game of rackets, fully occupy the morning from daylight, at which I invariably rise, until dinner, 5 o'clock. It is in the evening that *ennui* becomes a guest, for there is no society except of the few officers composing the detachment, for instance, a German, a Piedmontese, a Corsican, &c.

So long have I been accustomed to foreigners [he adds in another letter] that my native language seems of little use—French and Italian are our only languages now. I shall soon forget my native tongue. Would I could have some lessons in it from you!

I am absolutely *remarkable* in the regiment for the number and the length of the letters I write, and also for various translations from foreign papers.

His copious note-books full of poetry, and many extracts from books of history, bear witness to his love of reading.

Since I last wrote [this to his brother in April 1807] we have been on the point of attack. . . . On 1 March a division of about 2,500 or 3,000 French troops under General Merlin embarked . . . from Baiae and were half-way across, when a tempest arose which obliged them to put back. . . . We had only at most 700 men, and it requires 2,000 to guard all the landing-places, but I do not think we should have lost the island. We have worked night and day to increase our strength. . . . I often wished for practice in fortification; I have now plenty of it, as Colonel Lowe has made me chief engineer and inspector of the coast, and I have the whole of the fortifications for Ana Capri to design and complete with my own resources and according to my own ideas. Since we heard of M. Merlin's intentions we have considerably increased our ammunition. . . . By offering rewards for the balls fired by the British ships into the island when the place was taken, and which were to be found in the vineyards, I have recruited as far as 500 extra rounds; . . . since that we have received from Messina a large supply of ammunition and provisions, and we only wish to see our friends [the French].

Lowe manages so well that in spite of precautions we have almost daily correspondence with Naples, and are informed of everything going on there.

Italy is like a barrel of gunpowder, and only wants a match to blow it all up: that match is an English army of 20,000 men under Moore.

If the English at Capri managed to get wind of the enemy's movements, the scent of English doings at Capri was at least equally burning at the Court of Naples, and the intrigues of the French and of Queen Caroline of Sicily compelled the garrison to keep a strict watch on the inhabitants. 'This is a rascally island,' wrote Church in 1807, 'as you will see by this report of mine to Colonel Lowe. I have arrested some priests detected in correspondence with the French. This is a nuisance, for we are now obliged to fortify against the inhabitants on shore as well as against the enemy at sea.' The island seems to have been left by our commander-in-chief strangely unprotected at sea, considering its advanced and exposed position.

Six months without a ship-of-war of any sort, our greatest distance from the enemy's head-quarters being only eighteen miles, nearest two miles. My detachment and myself have had the hardest duty I ever experienced— watching and patrolling night after night, and working in the day-time: an enemy without, treason within, is enough to keep one on the alert. Enough of this vile island.

During 1808 the monotony of his island service was relieved by employment on expeditions along the Calabrian coast, watching and gaining information of the enemy's movements. He even seems to have been to Naples, doubtless in disguise, and to have been imprisoned there for four days on account of a dispute with a French officer; and he was sent with despatches to Messina to the commander-in-chief with a report of the affair.

So long as Church commanded at Ana Capri the rock was safe. But two events happened in the course of 1808 which materially affected the issues of the contest. Joseph Buonaparte was succeeded by Murat, and those who knew the two men were aware that this meant a complete change in the conduct of the war—a change from languor to masterly activity. The other event was the reinforcement of the garrison of Capri by the royal regiment of Malta—an increase merely in numbers, for the Maltese were not fit to stand in the shoes of the Corsicans, and the issue demonstrated the blunder of placing such troops at the post of danger. One important effect of the change was to transfer the command of Ana Capri to Major Hamill, who now occupied the advanced position with the Malta regiment, while Church and his Corsicans joined Hudson Lowe in Capri. The relief took place on 10 September, and the French were not slow to turn it to their own advantage. Church had been longing for an attack, though he knew that if the island were taken ' I should get into such a passion as to fight to the last rather than let the monsieurs have it without paying for it more than it is worth.' But now he had lost hope of a scrimmage. 'There is no chance of our being attacked,' he wrote, 'as at present we have two regiments here; I kept the place for two years with one' (26 September). Only a week after this confident assertion a large flotilla sailed from Naples with 3,000 men under Lamarque. The French attacked the island on all sides (4 October), but were vigorously repulsed by Hudson Lowe from the lower town. Ana Capri was less fortunate, and less well defended. Church and his Corsicans were ordered up to support the Maltese, but these had already allowed the enemy to land, under cover of the guns of a considerable flotilla, including a frigate, sloop-of-war, mortar vessel, and twenty-four gun-boats, which kept up a perpetual cannonade against the heights, under which their men ascended to the summit. In spite of their superior numbers the French were four times driven back with loss, and at sunset they had apparently made up their minds to return on board, for they were seen hiding among the rocks at the landing-place. In the evening, however, they were reinforced by other troops, who had been repulsed from Lower Capri, and as the moon rose Church saw three formidable columns advancing over the plain of Orico upon the town of Ana Capri. He kept up a brisk fire on their flank, but could not pursue as he found another body of the enemy threatening his right. The Malta regiment precipitately retired, the French passed through the lines, Church and his company of Corsicans were separated from the two other companies of his regiment; defence of Ana

Capri was already hopeless, and the enemy's guns could be heard in the town. All that remained was a perilous retreat. Church flung his guns into the sea, and guided his men through vineyards and narrow tracks towards Capo di Monte, whence a descent by steps led to Capri. On his road, to his intense surprise, for he had imagined the French at some distance, he suddenly fell in with a strong division of the enemy, and was instantly challenged. With prompt presence of mind he answered in French that his party were French troops pushing on to the town, and was allowed to proceed, the Corsicans actually brushing the enemy as they passed. Some of the Malta regiment in the rear, however, by their red uniforms betrayed the deception, and the result was a brisk fire, which pursued them for a mile. At last Church got his men, closely followed by the enemy, to Capo di Monte, and thence to Monte Salaro, picking up the two missing companies on the way. Here a letter from Hudson Lowe determined him to continue his retreat to Capri.

The adventures of the night were not yet over. To reach Lower Capri, where Lowe held his ground, was impossible unless the cliffs, some 150 feet high, and nearly perpendicular, were scaled. His local knowledge served him well in this emergency. The ordinary step-road was held by the French, but he knew of a path, scarcely practicable indeed, save to mountaineers, but such as Corsicans might compass; and down went the whole regiment, man by man, ammunition, guns, and all, in the blackness of night. It was a perilous descent, but only one man missed his footing; the rest with their officers joined Colonel Lowe at Capri the same night.

The French had won the day by a surprise, largely due to the supineness of the Malta regiment, but Church and the Corsicans enjoyed the full measure of praise for their daring. 'Captain Church's exertions,' reported Hudson Lowe, 'were peculiarly conspicuous. The orderly retreat of this detachment, through parties of the enemy and down precipices heretofore deemed impracticable, forms the highest eulogium on the officers who guided it. They had been twenty hours under arms and in constant movement.'

For a fortnight the garrison in Lower Capri held out against the slow siege of the French, who did not venture on an assault. For twelve nights and days the garrison was perpetually under arms. The reinforcements despatched by Sir John Stuart from Sicily were impeded by calms or dispersed by gales, and meanwhile ammunition ran short and a successful assault became imminent. When the enemy offered honourable terms of capitulation, Colonel Lowe had no alternative but to accept them (18 Oct.), and to withdraw his force to Sicily.[7] It was a severe blow to the British fame, and grievously weakened the effect of Maida. The French had enjoyed every advantage: an English frigate had retired before them, no sufficient succour had been attempted, the weather had been unprecedentedly calm for the time of year and had allowed a singularly easy disembarkation of troops and guns, and then changing to a gale prevented the arrival of British reinforcements; while the regiment at the point of attack had proved unequal to its duties. Nevertheless it was a calamity which the English burned to retrieve.

Church had been wounded in the head by a splinter from the last shot fired by the enemy (15 Oct.), while he was leading the sharp-shooters of Capri, and was put on board ship in a disabled state. On his arrival in Sicily he became the hero of the hour, and was warmly welcomed by the Commander-in-Chief and recommended for the majority in the Malta regiment, vacant by Major Hamill's death. He never joined the regiment, however, for he was soon well enough to ride across the island to Messina, where he was placed under Bunbury as assistant-quartermaster-general.

[7] See *Papers presented to the House of Commons relating to the capture of the Isle of Capri by the French Forces*. (Ordered to be printed March 29, 1809.)

CHAPTER IV.

THE IONIAN ISLANDS.

1809-1814.

How to retrieve the loss of Capri was the anxious thought of the British commanders in the Mediterranean, and especially of Lord Collingwood, who had succeeded Nelson in the command of the fleet. An expedition was despatched in the summer of 1809 to the Bay of Naples to make a reconnaissance 'for a particular object,'[*] but though Ischia and Procida were taken, and many of Murat's gun-boats captured, the movement was apparently a feint to deceive the enemy as to our real intentions. Church, who was honourably selected (27 June) to accompany the reconnaissance on board the *Canopus*, was sorely disappointed that no attempt was made to recover Capri, but subsequent proceedings restored his equanimity. In September the fleet sailed again from Sicily under sealed orders, the purport of which was unknown even to him (he was now assistant-quartermaster-general and chief of the staff to General Oswald, who commanded the troops of the expedition), and, instead of carrying on the usual operations against the Italian coasts, boldly sailed for the Adriatic and attacked the Ionian islands, then occupied by the French. The islanders had already sent urgent appeals to Collingwood and Stuart for English aid, and the result was the despatch of the 35th regiment, the Corsican rangers under Hudson Lowe, two companies of the 44th, a few dragoons, and a company of artillery, with the co-operation of H.M.S. *Warrior* (Captain Spranger) and other vessels. The first point of attack was Zante, where the French, taken completely by surprise, capitulated on the spot. Church conducted the landing, and drew up the terms of surrender (2 Oct.). Thenceforward, until the cession of Corfu by the French in 1814, Zante was the headquarters of the British government in the islands. Cephalonia

---

[*] Despatch from Lt.-Col. Collin, D.Q.M.G., to Capt. Church, June 27, 1809.

fell two days later to the onslaught of Colonel Lowe, and the reduction of Ithaca, in which Church himself commanded (supported by Captain Crawley of the *Philomel*) and 'made the French commander surrender unconditionally,' and of Cerigo, which had long been a nest of privateers, speedily followed, each in a single day.[9]

For five years the young officer's life (he was only twenty-six) was spent in active employment in the Ionian islands. It was work that was in every way suited to his special capacity; it tended more than any other experience to confirm the high opinion which he had, from the very first contact, formed of the Greeks, and which moulded the whole course of his later life. His genius lay in the command and discipline of native regiments; he seemed to possess a potent charm which gave him ascendency over rough and untutored ragamuffins, whom none but he could convert into something like orderly troops. Hardly had he arrived on the shores of Greece when he began to prepare for the levy of native regiments. His zealous enterprise in anticipating the requirements of his government led him immediately to prosecute a series of inquiries into the condition and resources of the Ionian islands and the adjacent mainland, and to report the results, illustrated by plans and maps of Corfu, Zante, Santa Maura, &c., to General Coffin at Messina. The information was especially welcome just then, for there were rumours, as an intercepted letter from the Morea to Buonaparte afterwards disclosed, that England contemplated the occupation of the Peloponnesus as a *place d'armes* against France; and a despatch from General Coffin (16 Jan. 1810), commending Church's zeal and discretion, emphasised the importance of his continuing to furnish reports, especially on the resources and disposition of the Moreotes, and the possibility of defending the isthmus of Corinth. The detailed report did not come in till many months later, and meanwhile the idea of an occupation had been abandoned; but it is full of minute information as to the proportions of Turks and Greeks in the Morea, and the probable number of fighting men, all of which proved of the utmost service to Church in his later dealings with the Greeks.

His observations of the qualities of the Greeks soon strengthened his estimate of their capabilities as soldiers, and in 1810–11 he was hard at work raising a force of 950 men. The first regiment of the duke of York's Greek light infantry was soon

---

[9] Despatches from Brig.-Gen. Oswald and Capt. Church, A.Q.M.G., in *London Gazette*, 16322, Dec. 5-9, 1809.

placed upon its trial. For three months the army in the Ionian
islands was left without a word of instructions from head-quarters
at Messina, and did not know what to do next: a delay, wrote
Church, 'characteristic of the manner in which we generally carry
on military matters.' In March 1811, however, it was decided to
attack the island of Santa Maura, and Church led his Greek
recruits to the assault of 'that diabolical castle seated like a
magician's fortress in the middle of the sea.' The new regiment
behaved with great steadiness and pluck, and the fort was taken;
but in the moment of victory Church's sabre was smashed by
grape, and his left arm was at the same instant shattered by a
bullet.[10] For two months he was seriously ill, for the bone was
divided, but a sound constitution and a skilful surgeon pulled him
through, and in the summer of 1811 he was allowed to go on leave
for a tour through Greece to Turkey and Asia Minor. With two
companions he rode through Northern Greece, Thessaly, and Macedonia, visiting Delphi, Chaeroneia, Thermopylae, Pharsalia, Philippi,
and other homes of classical associations; at Constantinople he
found a hospitable welcome at the embassy, and began a life-
long friendship with Stratford Canning, the twenty-four-year-old
minister at the Porte; while a row up the Bosphorus to the mur-
muring rocks of Jason, and an excursion to Smyrna and Magnesia,
completed a tour replete with intense interest to Church's romantic
imagination.

On his return he devoted himself again to the duties of his
Greek infantry. He had been appointed major commanding the
regiment early in 1810 by Sir John Stuart, for whom he always
testified a warm admiration and esteem: 'I look up to him as a
father,' he wrote home (12 Nov. 1811), '(a sacred name not to be
adopted without good cause); it is difficult to conceive the affection
he has for me; believe me, mother, it was a cordial to my grateful
heart to receive his unlimited approbation to my exertions on his
reviewing my regiment, which he did some time ago whilst on a
tour to these islands.' It remained to be seen, however, whether
Sir John's appointment would be ratified by the Horse Guards:
'Sir D. Dundas,' said Church, 'may have some of the MacSyco-
phant family to provide for, whose campaigns in England may

---

[10] What was thought at the Horse Guards of this exploit may be judged from a
letter from Sir H. E. Bunbury to Church, Aug. 9, 1810, in which he hoped his arm
was mending and that he might ' be able to enjoy the high credit you have so nobly
gained, without any alloy of sickness.'

entitle them to promotion prior to those sons of St. Patrick whose services are confined to the Mediterranean.' He was not fond of Scotsmen, and made unfavourable comments on the Highland regiments in Sicily. His fears, however, were groundless, and in November 1811 he was able to write, 'I am now full and approved major in His Majesty's service, and commanding a regiment originally raised, organised, and disciplined by myself,' where he had gained 'the warm approbation of my superiors, and the decided love and attachment of those placed under my command. My constant prayer is that I may be allowed to be of service to mankind and particularly to my country.' His letters are full of patriotic fervour, strong family love, and simple unaffected piety.

The command of the regiment taxed Church's powers to the utmost. He was far from well; his wound was still open, after a year and a half; and his visit to Turkey had been followed by a severe and distressing fever. Moreover, the management of raw Greek levies was a very different matter from a parade in Wellington Barracks.

You will conceive [he told his mother, 12 Nov. 1811] that my charge is no light one—that of a thousand men—and that my mind is continually occupied with the cares, the necessary attendants of so heavy a trust; for do not conceive that I have the easy task of an officer in command of an English regiment where all is clock-work, and where the men are accustomed to the rules of discipline. Far different has been my task, and through the Almighty's assistance I have been enabled to reduce to obedience and military discipline men whom English, Russians, or French, could never in any way discipline or civilise. To you, mother, I do not boast; but I have now, thank God, divested those men of prejudices rooted by ages, and converted them from the most lawless of mankind, not only into good soldiers, but also into praiseworthy members of civilised society. These men, who once knew no law but their sword, are now the admiration of the inhabitants for their correct, quiet, and obedient conduct. My maxim has been to treat them with mildness and humanity, and by that means I have succeeded in gaining the love of these people beyond what can be imagined. The number of recruits that flock to me from all parts of Greece is really extraordinary. . . . Should government wish for men, I will answer from my character alone in this country to raise 6,000 or 8,000 men in as many months. The regiment is now regularly approved of by government, and will enjoy the same advantages as all other in His Majesty's service.

General Oswald was much impressed with the ability displayed by his chief of the staff in recruiting the regiment. 'The first embodiment of the Greeks in our service,' he wrote, 21 Aug. 1811, 'was one of those delicate experiments demanding a rare and unusual combination of conciliation and firmness, and indeed of that enthusiasm by which great difficulties alone can be overcome. No one,' he added, 'was so capable of embodying and disciplining people whose love and respect you had by the most valid titles acquired,' and he not only assured Church that the regiment would remain under his command, but that he might look forward to the formation of a second regiment of the same kind which would also be placed under his orders as lieutenant-colonel. 'For my own part,' said the general, 'I am convinced that our corps is but the commencement of a great plan for engaging numbers of Greeks in our service.'

The wheels of government roll slowly, and it was not at once that these predictions were realised. Church, however, lost no time in making preparations for embodying another Greek regiment so soon as permission should arrive from home. Considerable enthusiasm had been aroused in the Morea by the success of the first experiment, and numerous offers of assistance came in from the chiefs, insomuch that the Turkish authorities took alarm, and complained of what they imagined might be construed as an infraction of their neutrality towards France. Volunteers wrote from all parts of Greece, and their letters possess a singular interest in view of later events. They show that the Greeks were already looking to England as their champion against the misrule of the Turks, and they also bear witness to the eagerness of the Greeks to profit by the advantages of English discipline, which they plainly foresaw would turn to their profit in the deadly struggle which was already flashing upon their horizon. The Greek regiments raised by Church in the Ionian Islands took no small part in the War of Independence; the names of Colocotroni, Valaeti, Vlacopoulo, Stratto, and other prominent leaders in the revolution, figure among his recruits at Zante; and his influence over the men was the direct cause of their eager desire to serve under him again in their effort for freedom in 1827. They had grown to love him in the earlier years at Zante, when they served as mercenaries of a foreign power, and would have no other leader when they fought for their own homes.

How strong and beloved that influence was, may be gathered from the memorial (24 July 1812) which the first regiment of Greek light infantry presented to their major on his departure for

England on sick-leave, for his wound still troubled him. They recited their experience of three years' service under his orders, and spoke of his success as a 'zealous, benevolent, and mild' commander, who had 'won them by affection from their own country to learn military science' under his direction, and had even converted those who had always maintained that the Greeks were incapable of discipline. Among those who signed this memorial were names conspicuous under the same leader in the War of Independence.

There was no doubt that the experiment had succeeded; and even the Horse Guards, after a period of bewildered surprise, were free to express their entire satisfaction with the zeal and enthusiasm of the young major, who was now pleading his cause in person at Whitehall. All the authorities concurred in admiration of his energy and tact; the duke of York, commander-in-chief, was 'fully impressed with the judicious and zealous conduct he had invariably manifested in the command and organisation of the Greek light infantry;'[11] and the recommendations of Sir J. Stuart, Generals Campbell and Airey, and Colonels Bunbury and Torrens, induced the home authorities to waive the objection of his youth and brief period of service, and to create a special second lieutenant-colonelcy expressly for him in the 1st Greek light infantry.[12] Moreover, the commander-in-chief, alive to the importance of Colonel Church's recruiting abilities, favourably entertained and supported his memorial and offer to raise a second corps like the first.[13] A despatch from Lord Palmerston to Church (War Office, 29 June, 1813) gave the necessary permission and regulations for the new regiment, which was to be officered by Greeks, with the exception of the lieutenant-colonel and one British captain. The men of Sparta, Elis, Epirus, Arcadia, Aetolia, Messene, Acarnania, and the Islands, came forward with enthusiasm, and the regiment was speedily embodied at Cephalonia to the permitted strength—first of 450, and subsequently of 580 men, with English staff and field officers. The corps was engaged for five years and for service in any part of Europe, but the only action in which it took part was the capture of Paxo on 14 Feb. 1814; when, by skilful combination with Captain Taylor of the *Apollo*, Church and

---

[11] Despatch from H. Torrens to R. Church, Feb. 26, 1813.
[12] H. Torrens to R. Church, Horse Guards, Nov. 25, 1812.
[13] Despatch from Frederick, Comm.-in-Chief, to Lt.-Col. Church, March 9, 1813 and from the same to Earl Bathurst, April 27, 1813.

Arata surprised the citadel.[14] A garrison order of 8 July, 1814, gives a very favourable report of the steadiness and soldierlike bearing of the 2nd Greek light infantry, and its good conduct throughout its year of service; but its work was now over. The general peace put an end to all military operations in the Mediterranean: the Greek regiments were disbanded[15] in October, partly in deference to the representations of Turkey;[16] and the men returned quietly and in excellent spirits to their homes.[17] To Church personally the disbanding was a severe pecuniary loss; he had spent considerable sums in recruiting, and lost his pay and appointments after a single year's tenure.

The Septinsular Republic was now revived under the protection of Great Britain, and the officer who had taken so large a share in its recovery and organisation was summoned to Vienna to lay before the Congress of Europe a report on the conditions and resources of the islands. The report is an excellent summary of the strategical and commercial importance of Corfu as a possession of Great Britain, and upon it the Ionian treaty was largely founded. This closed the fourth period of Colonel Church's services. His connexion with the Ionian Islands terminated amid the cordial congratulations of the commander-in-chief, the general in command, and all others in authority. He had played an important part in the organisation of the Septinsular Republic, which for half a century formed a valuable and legitimate field for British influence in the Mediterranean.

[14] Lt.-Col. Church to Lt.-Gen. J. Campbell, Paxo, Feb. 15, 1814.
[15] General Order, Corfu, Sept. 14, 1814.
[16] Lt.-Gen. J. Campbell to Lt.-Col. Church, Zante, Nov. 8, 1813.
[17] General Orders, Argostoli, Oct. 1; Corfu, Oct. 25, 1814.

CHAPTER V.

THE ARMY OF ITALY.

1813–1816.

FROM 1814 to 1820 Church's energies were diverted into a new channel, where he found even more scope for his passion for adventure than in the hazards of Capri or the training of Greek brigands. Had he pursued the ordinary course of service in the English army, there can be no doubt that he would have risen to high command; but his nature was altogether opposed to such monotonous advance. He loved peril and adventure; he delighted in feeling his power over undisciplined mountaineers, and seeing raw recruits of the most unpromising appearance grow under his keen yet sympathetic eye into orderly and steady troops. The command of the Corsican Rangers had accustomed him to dealing with such materials, and the levy of the Greek regiment at Zante had perfected his experience. To give up such exciting and responsible work for the routine of an English parade-ground, now that the Peninsular war was over, was repugnant to his energetic nature; and so we find him taking service where there was plenty to be done and seen, and where he soon had an opportunity of extending his experience in managing men who lived in open contempt of all authority. The particular direction now taken was due in a large measure to a new influence which had come upon him, and which for many years reigned over his enthusiastic and loyal disposition. This influence belonged to Count Nugent, an English officer attached first to the Austrian and then to the Neapolitan service, who seems to have been the Prince Rupert of the southern campaigns against Buonaparte—a man of high mettle, beloved by his comrades, eager for battle, and carrying with him that good fortune which often accompanies brilliant audacity.

Church was already intimately acquainted with Nugent when he joined him at Vienna in 1813. On his way back to the Ionian

Islands after his absence on leave in England, the young lieutenant-colonel of Greek light infantry was entrusted by Lord Castlereagh [14] with a political mission to Constantinople, with orders to go by way of Vienna and on his road to visit the chief armies of the allies. He had begun with Sweden, where he travelled from Gottenburg to Ystad; and then, crossing to Stralsund, met his old friend Sir Hudson Lowe, and Sir Charles (afterwards Lord) Stewart, Lord Castlereagh's brother, in whose company he witnessed a review of Arenschild's Russo-German legion, and drank a bumper to Wellington for his triumph at Vittoria. Passing through Berlin, he arrived at Vienna in August, where Lord Cathcart received him very graciously, and gave him a commission as flattering as it was agreeable, though it practically superseded his original route to Constantinople. 'He has directed me,' wrote Church to Colonel Bunbury (11 Aug. 1813), 'to proceed to join General Nugent, with whom I am at present here. We leave to-day for Agram, and the corps under his command is destined to open the communication with the Adriatic. After the communication is opened I shall proceed to Zante, and return from thence to the continent, bringing with me such troops as General Campbell may spare, together with my *own* men, and also leaving proper officers for the recruiting of the regiment and the forwarding them to us as speedily as possible; and I reckon upon good service from them even in an undisciplined state.' This was just the sort of vigorous work he enjoyed, and he looked forward with his usual sanguine hopefulness to a brilliant campaign under the man for whom he had already conceived a strong affection. As usual, too, he spent what he could in aiding the public cause. 'I am likely to be the first British officer employed actively in this service, adding also my inconsiderable means to it. I am sanguine enough to trust that my exertions will not fail to gain me credit in the field.' He had not, however, advanced far into Croatia when matters began to assume a less rosy hue. He wrote to Colonel Bunbury from Carlstadt (20 Aug. 1813), 'I confess I am thunderstruck with the appearance and system of the Austrian generals whom I have seen, nor can I augur anything favourable from their proceedings. If those in Bohemia are not better than the gentlemen I have seen hitherto, I candidly confess I have no wish to serve with them. I believe our friend General Nugent feels these things as much as I do, and sees them in the same light.

---

[14] Lord Castlereagh to Lieut.-Col. Church, 1 Aug. 1813.

'... If he extricates himself altogether from their hands, something may be done, but as long as he remains under their orders nothing brilliant can possibly take place.... I have never suffered so much *ennui* in my life as since I have mixed with and become a companion of the Austrian officers. *I could say a great deal about everybody, but I dare not.* ... Having nothing to do, I am more like a spectator, a situation the most abominable of all others. ... The Austrian army amounts to 260,000 men, neither more nor less. The soldiers and people are enthusiastic, and bitter enemies of the French; but how they will be conducted by their chief, God knows!'

As it happened, none of the things he dreaded came to pass. The Austrians under Nugent, by a series of rapid marches and brilliant surprises, drove the enemy from before Carlstadt, occupied Fiume (26 Aug.) with only 1,500 men, and opened communications with the British fleet under Admiral Fremantle in the Adriatic.[19] Church then left for Zante to draw off a contingent of troops for the Italian campaign, but men could not be spared.[20] The 2nd Greek regiment, however, as we have seen,[21] was raised and placed under his command, Paxo was taken, and then came the general peace, and the services of the Ionian regiments were no longer needed. On the conclusion of an armistice with Murat in February Church was sent to Naples[22] to negotiate on the situation of Corfu, which was shortly afterwards surrendered to Great Britain; and after disbanding the Greek regiments he was summoned by Lord Cathcart in November 1814 to make his report on the Ionian Islands to the Congress of Vienna. He was still there when the news of Buonaparte's escape from Elba, in the spring of 1815, dropped like a bomb in the midst of the stately ceremonies of that portentous conclave. Among the various hurried dispositions which ensued, the influence of Nugent made itself felt in Church's destination. At the count's special request he was appointed to accompany him as British military resident with the Austrian army during the campaign against Murat in Italy, and subsequently against the army of Provence. His reports from head-quarters to Lord Stewart at Vienna[23] have been preserved, and form a con-

---

[19] Church to Lord Cathcart, Carlstadt, 20 Aug., Fiume, 27 Aug. 1813; to Lord W. Bentinck, Zante, 23 Sept. 1813.

[20] Church to Lord W. Bentinck, Zante, 23 Sept. 1813.   [21] *Supra*, p. 29.

[22] Lieut.-General J. Campbell to Church, Zante, 9 Feb. 1814.

[23] To Lord Stewart, head-quarters, Mantua, 23 April; Serravalle, 30 April; Rome, 3, 5, 9, and 11 May; Arce, 15 May; San Germano, 17 May; Caijanello, 18 May; Aversa, 21 May; Naples, 22 May, 1815.

nected narrative of a short, little-known campaign, in which (April–May 1815) Murat's army was driven from Mantua all the way to Naples. When he arrived on the scene of action he found Bianchi's and Neyperg's divisions of the imperial army of Italy, under Frimont as commander-in-chief, already in the thick of the fray. Murat and the Neapolitan troops had been defeated on the Tanaro, and forced to abandon the whole line of the Po. Nugent, commanding Bianchi's advance guard, was pursuing Murat with his usual dash towards Rimini. Step by step the Austrians and Tuscans, in a series of small engagements, pressed 'King Joachim' southward, while Nugent and Church, marching, with their customary rapidity, 100 miles in three days, occupied Rome and prepared for the advance upon Naples. The usurper's army was gradually melting away; 400,000 had dwindled to 10,000, and when Nugent with but a tenth of their numbers forced battle on the Neapolitans at Miguano, near San Germano, hardly 700 escaped to announce the destruction of the 'Army of the Interior.' The remnant capitulated at Capua; Murat took to flight; and the imperial army escorted Prince Leopold of Sicily into Naples amidst the plaudits of the fickle inhabitants (22 May 1815). The campaign had been full of interest and excitement, and Church had himself specially contributed to its success by raising 5,000 recruits in Rome, where he enjoyed the curious distinction of being sole military commander for over a fortnight. His conduct received the unqualified approval of the general commanding the forces in Sicily, and the thanks of the king; he was decorated with the order of the Fleur de Lys; and created a *maresciallo di campo* (major-general) by his restored Neapolitan majesty, Ferdinand IV.

Hardly was this business over when Bianchi and Nugent were sent to Provence to put down the remains of Buonapartism there, and to moderate the excesses of the royalists, who were exacting sanguinary reprisals from the vanquished. Church accompanied the army in the same capacity as before, from July to November 1815. Landing at Nice, he found the whole country roused to indignation by the barbarities of the Buonapartists under Marshal Brune, the same who was said to have exhibited the head of the beautiful and unfortunate princesse de Lamballe to Marie Antoinette on the point of a pike at the window of her prison in the Temple. Church confirmed the story of his atrocities,[24] and no one seems

---

[24] Despatch to Lord Burghersh, head-quarters, Nice, 21 July 1815.

to have been very sorry when Brune was lynched by the people of Avignon.

Little of importance marked the occupation of the south of France.[25] The garrison of Antibes was composed of staunch Buonapartists, who refused to surrender. They were the same men who had lately erected a monument on the shore of the bay of Jouan, hard by, to commemorate the spot where Buonaparte had landed on his return from Elba. Bianchi besieged the garrison, and Church razed the monument. Under it was found a box containing a report of the commemorative ceremony, signed by all the officers of the 87th and 106th regiments (who thereby solemnly pledged themselves to the emperor's cause), together with coins, stars, and eagles of the Legion of Honour. The copper tablet on the monument, which was given to Church, and is still in the possession of the family, bore this inscription, rudely cut:

> NAPOLÉON TRAHI S'ÉLOIGNA DU TRÔNE
> ET SE RETIRA À L'ÎLE D'ELBE.
> RAPPELÉ PAR LES VŒUX DE LA NATION,
> C'EST ICI QU'IL DÉBARQUA LE 1ᴇʀ MARS 1815.
> LE 87ᴱᴹᴱ REGIMENT LUI ÉRIGEA CE MONUMENT.[26]

Provence was then overrun by foreign troops. Sir Hudson Lowe commanded the British land force at Marseilles; Lord Exmouth and the Mediterranean squadron co-operated with Bianchi along the coast; the latter's advance guard under Nugent was already within the French border. Church perceived, with that ready sympathy for the unfortunate which was one of his leading characteristics, that the luckless Provençaux, most of whom were loyal to the old order, were driven to the brink of ruin by the successive incursions of Buonapartist and royalist armies, and he immediately despatched vigorous remonstrances to Lord Castlereagh at Paris, urging him to have Bianchi's orders cancelled and the Austrian army stopped at the frontier. What success he had at headquarters is uncertain; but his direct appeal to Bianchi had the de-

---

[25] Despatches to Lord Burghersh, Cannes, 24 July; to Lord Castlereagh, Cannes, 25 July; Marseilles, 28 July; Aix, 1 Aug.; Marseilles, 4, 5, 12, 16 Aug.; Aix, 27 Aug.; Avignon, 29 Aug.; Nismes, 30, 31 Aug.; to Lord Exmouth, Avignon, 31 Aug.; to the senior officer of the fleet, Avignon, 1 Sept.; to Lord Castlereagh, Avignon, 2 Sept.; to Colonel Burrows, Avignon, 8 Sept.; to Lord Exmouth, Avignon, 14 Sept.; to Lord Castlereagh, Avignon, 15, 18, 19 Sept., 4, 15 Oct.; to J. Planta, Marseilles, 20 Oct.; to Lord Castlereagh, Marseilles, 24, 29 Oct. 1815.

[26] To Lord Castlereagh, Cannes, 25 July 1815.

sired effect: the order to advance was recalled, and Provence was saved from further exactions.

Before this, in August, he and Nugent accompanied Lord Exmouth on a visit of inspection to the French arsenal at Toulon. They saw twenty-four ships of the line, and twelve or fourteen frigates; 'not one of which is in a state to go to sea,'[27] since only one of them had any rigging. Nor were there many guns; in fact, 'the arsenal seems to me almost destitute of the means of equipping a squadron of three or four sail of the line.' Soon after this visit Nugent left France to take command of the Austrian troops at Naples, and, as Bianchi's army also evacuated Avignon, Church's commission came to an end. A letter from Lord Castlereagh (18 Oct. 1815) conveyed permission to return to England, and the Prince Regent's 'entire approbation of the manner in which he had performed the duties of the missions with which he had been entrusted.' He had shortly before received the decoration of a Companion of the Bath, in common with a few other distinguished officers, who had been similarly employed as residents with the continental armies —among them Sir H. (afterwards viscount) Hardinge and Colonel Leake, well known as the topographer of Greece.

What Church was doing during the next year or two can only be gathered from a few letters. He was still at Marseilles in November 1815, for there he received a very friendly note from Lord Exmouth, strongly advising him to stick to Naples, 'under Nugent's wing,' and thus to keep his name before the Austrian authorities, who were sure to hold the predominant influence in Italy for some time at least; and proposing a meeting at Leghorn and a month together at Rome. But a call from his general drew him now to Naples, where he had already received the title of major-general in the Neapolitan army. A letter at this time from his old colonel, Hudson Lowe, mentions the consent of the Horse Guards to Church's Neapolitan appointment: he adds, 'I am going out to St. Helena—wide as the poles asunder! I hope, however, not for any long period.' Church was evidently attracted by Lord Exmouth's impetuous character, and must have sought to share in the vigorous action taken by the admiral in the spring of 1816 for the suppression of slavery in the Barbary states. It was just the work he would have relished, and, in sending home more than 1,100 Sicilian and Neapolitan slaves, Lord Exmouth wrote to him as to a trusted sympathiser—

[27] To Lord Burghersh, Marseilles, 12 Aug. 1815.

Boyne, off Lampedosa: 1 May 1816.

My dear Church,—I will not permit the transport with the last of the slaves from Tripoli to proceed to Naples without giving you my farewell from the Mediterranean for old England. I have to call only at Algiers, where I should rejoice to give them a lesson from the sides of the old *Boyne.* If I dare act, as I wish, my only hope is of meeting some orders from home which may allow me to go further than I have done. I am sure there is but one feeling amongst us all, from the flag to the keel. We have obtained from Tunis and Tripoli signed declarations that they will make, or rather keep, no more slaves, but, in case of war, exchange prisoners and treat them with humanity and in the same manner as European nations. I think we have released about twenty-four or twenty-five hundred, and shipped them off at once. . . . You will laugh when I tell you the Bey of Tripoli, who has murdered his father and brother with some half-score cousins, absolutely cried like a child the morning his slaves embarked. We had four who slept in his room for years from fear: for you must know that his conscience troubles him in his dreams. God bless you! I repeat no offers of friendship, having done so in my last, and I wish you to believe me sincere, and that I am, my dear Church, with great truth and regard,

Your faithful friend and servant,

Exmouth.

The admiral's desires about Algiers were soon gratified, and in August came the famous bombardment which ought to have put an end for ever to slavery in the deylik. Church must have been greatly disappointed that he was not with Lord Exmouth at the time; for by a despatch from the marquis de Circello, dated 13 Aug. 1816, he was appointed on a special mission for the king of Naples to accompany the English admiral, and to recover the Neapolitan prisoners then in confinement, and obtain certain advantages for the kingdom of the Two Sicilies. It sounds very strange to us now that the Neapolitan government were bound by ancient treaty to pay to the dey of Algiers 20,000 dollars annually; but it is notorious that all the maritime powers of Europe had been in the habit of paying black-mail to the Barbary States ever since the days of Ochiali and the battle of Lepanto.[28] There were besides 600 or 700 Neapolitan slaves, for whom the ransom of 1,000 dollars a head was demanded. But Lord Exmouth's cannon had blown up existing treaties, and Church could not have been in time to join his friend in the deliverance of the prisoners, nor does it appear that he accepted the mission.

[28] See the writer's *Barbary Corsairs,* (1890), ch. xix.

CHAPTER VI.

THE BRIGANDS OF APULIA.

1817-20.

A NEW and arduous field of work now opened before him. The recovery of the crown by Ferdinand IV, or I of the Two Sicilies, had not been attended with propitious consequences. The king's treachery in the matter of the constitution, the jealousy of Murat's old officers, and the rivalries of Italians and Austrians, tended to paralyse the government and breed discontent throughout the provinces. Moreover the policy of encouraging secret societies in their war against the French now bore fruit; what had been used as a tool against Buonaparte now became a weapon against all constituted authority. The country was overrun by brigands of the most desperate character. Communications were interrupted; the roads were perilous to the last degree; government specie was intercepted; and, in spite of the deterrent effect of highwaymen's heads stuck up in the valley of Bovino, few travellers ventured to thread that gloomy pass to the Apulias. Canosa's foundation of the Calderari as a counterpoise to the Carbonari had done more harm than good; the new society only irritated the people and intimidated the magistrates, who found themselves surrounded by a new body of spies quite as dangerous as the 'good cousins' who levied blackmail on all the respectable inhabitants.[29]

In 1817 affairs had grown to a crisis. The secret societies were supreme in the land. Besides the Carbonari, who were sometimes honest politicians—like Gabriele Rossetti, the poet's father—and sometimes ruffians, there were such sects as the 'European Patriots' and the 'Philadelphi,' in themselves comparatively innocent of

---

[29] The materials for most of the facts related in this chapter are found in General Church's manuscript memoirs on the state of the Apulias, and in Baron Bertholdi's anonymous *Memoirs of the Carbonari* (Murray, 1821).

crime, though their members often belonged to more guilty associations. Worst of all was the company of the 'Decisi,' or 'Order of Jupiter Tonans,' a species of nihilists, vowed to the destruction of all existing institutions and the assassination of all obstructors. The records of this society, which were afterwards seized by Church, proved that their immediate objects were murder and plunder. No one could join unless he could boast of two murders committed with his own hand, and every member was pledged to assassinate any person whom the order might choose to condemn. If it was desired to get a rival or a creditor out of the way, all that was necessary was to apply to the Decisi, and pay a sufficient fee, when the man's life was not worth a week's purchase. The villains did their work neatly and with becoming solemnity, and, as at some sacred rite, accompanied by the blare of trumpets, plunged their daggers into their victim's heart *con vero entusiasmo*. Threatening letters formed part of their method, and lands and property of all sorts were annexed at the point of the dagger. Four dots added to a threatening letter secured instant obedience: for they signified death. As a symbol of their sanguinary character the diplomas of membership were written in blood.

The president of this dreaded society was the abbate Ciro Annichiarico, a priest of Grottaglie, who had begun his ecclesiastical career with the extermination of a neighbouring family, and had revenged himself for his consequent imprisonment by vowing war against all authority, human and divine, for the rest of his unnatural life. Ciro was one of those dazzling scoundrels whose daring and address are apt for the moment to make one forget their crimes. He was a splendid horseman and unerring shot; no danger cowed him, no risk was too great to be run. His fertility in disguise and marvellous adroitness in escape gave him the reputation of an enchanter, so that folk hardly dared to whisper his name for fear his imps should seize them; and true to his character, like Claverhouse, he is said to have met his death at last by the silver bullet. Women adored him, and he had a mistress in every town and village in the wide circuit of his depredations, who loved him none the less that he was an assassin of a dye as black as history or romance has ever painted.

He was now a man of forty, and for eighteen years had been the scourge of the Apulias—or the Terra di Bari and Terra di Otranto, to give them their modern names—when General Church was appointed, first to inquire into the state of the provinces, and then to take over the supreme command (1817). At that time there were at least 30,000 members of secret societies in the Apulias, many of whom, however, belonged more from fear than inclination; for it was well known that he who was not for the Decisi was counted as against them, and such did not dare to cross their own thresholds, lest they should meet the poniard. From twenty to twenty-five murders were taking place every week, many of them accompanied by details of a revolting nature. A beautiful girl, a princess, whose youth and beauty and total lack of protection should have been defence enough, was brutally murdered, and worse, in her own chamber, out of mere greed of gold. A band of ruffians was disguised as *policinelli*, and attended the village merrymakings, only to plunge their steel into their unsuspecting partners or boon fellows at the dance or evening carouse.

So far all efforts to suppress these terrible associations had been fruitless. The fault did not lie with the central government, which was for the moment exceptionally able. Canosa's successor, Don Luigi de' Medicis, the leading minister, was a man of talent, a scholar, and a gentleman; old Danero, the minister of the navy 'who slept every night of his life in his red pantaloons with his sword by his side,' ready for emergencies, and who lived to be 103, was the type of an honest if somewhat antique officer; Count Nugent was captain-general, and had immense influence with the king; and Church was inspector-general and commander of the foreign troops. All these were unaffectedly eager to restore order and Nugent and Church worked together in perfect trust and sympathy. Moreover, but for their jealousies and distrust of the king and government, the officers of the army were efficient and apparently trustworthy, and good materials for recruiting were at hand; while the *gendarmerie* proved themselves brave and steady under a leader who inspired confidence. But the local authorities were either the accomplices or the tools of the secret societies, who held their lives in their hands, and such of them as were really honest dared not stand forth without some better guarantee of protection than was then offered.

Towards the close of 1817 Church left Naples to take command of the terror-stricken provinces. He was furnished with a force of Neapolitan troops, of various nationalities, which was soon supplemented by a corps of his favourite Greeks; and early in 1818 he was granted the *alter ego*, or royal prerogative of life and death, by autograph letter from the king and upon the unanimous recommendation of the council of ministers.[30] At first people only thought that a new do-nothing had come among them; they had seen many generals, and none had yet proved a match for Don Ciro. But Church soon showed them that he was not made of Neapolitan stuff. His physique, though not commanding, gave an impression of great energy. He was described in 1820 as 'below the middle height, extremely well built, spare, sinewy, and active, with a well-proportioned head, sharp piercing eyes, rather aquiline nose, and a closely compressed mouth, denoting great firmness and resolution.'[31] But his perfect dauntlessness was perhaps the chief argument in his favour among a frightened population. They knew he carried his life in his hand every day, but he seemed to care as little for danger as if he had been dipped in Styx. Again and again he stood the brigands' fire with a smile of amusement; he ventured almost unattended into places noted as the ambushes of the outlaws, and fearlessly accepted the hospitality of persons who, he was warned, were the secret accomplices of Ciro and quite capable of mixing poison in his wine. Once he was surprised by a strong party of the Vardarelli, a body of brigands and political assassins, who boasted that they were the real sovereigns of the country, and nothing but his perfect *sang-froid* and contempt of danger carried him safely and even amicably through an interview which seemed fated to a bloody end. The people began to understand that they had a new sort of governor to deal with, and Annichiarico himself bit his thumb with spite, and swore, in his rather ambiguous slang, 'I have pooped lots of generals, French, Italian, and Neapolitan, but this fellow will end by pooping me!' The process took less time than the reverend outlaw imagined. One by one the authorities of the towns and villages threw off their allegiance to the secret societies and joined the cause of order; step by step Church narrowed the circle which he had drawn with his troops round the district affected by Ciro and his followers; one after the other the ruffians were caught and executed, and at last the desperate remnant of the gang and their leader were run to earth. The chase and capture of Ciro Annichiarico would fill a lively chapter. Brought at last before the court martial without which Church suffered no prisoner to be condemned, the felon was asked how many murders he had committed. 'Sixty

---

[30] Count Nugent to Church, Naples, 20 Feb. 1818.

[31] Sir J. Rennie, *Autobiography*, p. 55. The author was Church's guest at Lecce in 1820.

or seventy,' he answered carelessly, *E chi lo sa? saranno tra sessanta e settanta.* A priest offered him the last consolations, but Ciro laughed: *Lasciate queste chiacchiere; siamo dell' istessa professione; non ci burliamo fra noi.* Then on 8 Feb. 1818 he was led out to execution at Francavilla, in the presence of 40,000 people, and placed, like other malefactors, back to the firing party. Twenty-one shots took effect, and still he breathed; then, 'seeing that he was enchanted,' the soldiers gravely loaded his own gun with a silver ball, and the spell was immediately broken.

The spell was broken indeed throughout the provinces. As soon as the centre and soul of the organisation had paid the forfeit, his subordinates hastily submitted. 'A few months were sufficient,' said Church, ' to totally destroy the assassins and brigands, and to break up the different revolutionary societies, to receive the submission of their chiefs and the surrender of their arms.' How complete was the suppression may be gathered from the fact that, during the two years that Church continued to govern the Apulias after this decisive stroke, not a single instance of murder or brigandage occurred in a population of three-quarters of a million. The grateful people held solemn services of thanksgiving in every church in the provinces; a commemorative column was erected at Lecce, and the freedom of the city and the sword of honour were presented by the citizens to their deliverer. 'You seem to have come out most triumphantly,' wrote Sir W. A'Court (the English minister at Naples, afterwards Lord Heytesbury) to Church (Naples, 16 Sept. 1818), 'from a most delicate and perilous situation, and I can assure you that your merits in the exercise of the powers intrusted to you are fully appreciated here. I have reason to know that the king as well as the whole of his administration are in the highest degree sensible of the prudence and vigour which you have displayed.'

Impressed with the value of his services, the government of Naples resolved to keep a tight hold on him, and his requests for leave of absence to England were met by De' Medicis with affectionate assurances that, so far as his power went, he would not suffer Church to quit the kingdom, where his services were indispensable. In 1820 a fresh mark of the royal esteem towards him was shown in his appointment as governor of the district of Palermo and commander-in-chief of the army in Sicily, with the rank of lieutenant-general. *Je me flatte*, wrote De' Medicis, 22 March, *que vous verrez dans la nouvelle charge que le Roi vient de vous confier une preuve éclatante de la bienveillance de S.M. et de sa satisfaction pour le service que vous ne cessez de rendre avec un zèle et un empressement tout particuliers.* The appointment, however, did not prove auspicious: his career under the Neapolitan government was destined to end as suddenly and disastrously as its beginning had been rapid and triumphant. The shiftiness of the king and the intrigues of the Carbonari had allowed the germs of revolution to ferment. Church found the troops at Palermo radically disaffected, and either themselves Carbonari or fraternising with the sectaries. The garrison was altogether inadequate and quite untrustworthy; military discipline appeared to be unknown, and the soldiers wore the badges of the Carbonari in the streets. His own antecedents, as a resolute suppressor of secret societies, deprived him of all hold over the mass of the population. Hardly had the new commander arrived when news came of the revolution at Naples and the king's forced promulgation of the 'constitution of Spain.' The effect upon the Sicilians was instantaneous. Soldiers and civilians alike broke into open revolt, cheered the constitution, derided the king, and shouted for 'Robespierre' and the 'independence of Sicily.' A courageous attempt to restore order ended in threats against the general's life. Church was mobbed by armed fanatics, and when at last he entered a carriage and drove away, two aides-de-camp with drawn swords hardly availed to keep off the infuriated crowd, who pressed about the carriage, throwing stones, brandishing daggers, and shouting *Mori! mori!* Church himself was stunned by a stone, and an officer by his side was stabbed, before they effected their escape to the coast. All attempts to return to the scene of action proved futile and fraught with peril, and at length, with much reluctance, the general gave orders to sail for Naples, there to give an account of his proceedings to whatever authority he might find in power.[32]

He knew he was running into the lion's jaws, but he hardly realised how voraciously they would snap upon him. When he reached Naples he found the ministry overturned by the Carbonari and the king a prisoner. The royal flag was struck down as soon as the vessel was boarded by the officials, and Church was hurried away to the Castello dell' Ovo without being informed of any charge to be brought against him. He had verily fallen among thieves. 'The parliament,' wrote Sir W. A'Court, 'is composed of a set of

---

[32] General Sir Richard Church's 'Personal Narrative of the Revolution at Palermo,' in *Monthly Magazine*, Feb.-March 1826.

Carbonari scoundrels, over whom neither the prince nor his ministers have any more influence than you or I.' Indeed Church's return was exactly the Quixotic act of a chivalrous nature which might have been expected of him. 'I admire,' wrote A'Court again, ' the spirit of rectitude which brought you here, however I may lament the imprudence of your committing yourself into the hands of your enemies, and that in a moment of revolution, when reason and justice are hushed and nothing but the most malevolent passions in play. Why did you not go on board the frigate in the bay? . . . What can I do for you? How can I serve you? Remember I have *no power* now, no influence at all. . . I wish you had gone to Gaeta, as the prince proposed, but General Ramsay tells me you would not hear of it. . . It is an infamous business altogether. Campochiaro himself says he is ashamed of it.'

For six months the general who had deserved so well of Italy suffered the misery of a Neapolitan prison. In vain the British minister presented official remonstrances; in vain the English residents, including Lords Ruthven, Clarina, and Colchester, and other well-known names, petitioned (Sept. 1820) for his release. The only mitigation he was offered was to go out on parole, on condition of appearing at any moment before the commission which was to try his unknown crime, and this he indignantly refused. At length he was put upon a sort of trial, which ended in his acquittal (Jan. 1821) of whatever he was charged with, and it is not to be wondered that he shook off the dust of Naples from his feet in disgust and returned to England.

He lost his property in the revolution at Palermo and Naples, and received no recompense from the constitutional government. But amidst all the intrigues of parties he had upheld the English name by his straightforward honesty and simplicity of character, and it was no slight satisfaction to him, on his return to England, to receive from his own government a mark of their approbation. On 3 March 1822 he was made Knight Commander of the Royal Hanoverian Guelphic Order, ' in consideration of distinguished services, and in particular those which you have rendered in Germany and Italy since the year 1813, when appointed to attend the allied armies on the continent.'

CHAPTER VII.

THE WAR OF INDEPENDENCE.

1826–1827.

To STUDENTS of history Sir Richard Church's name is chiefly known in connexion with the operations of the Greek army during the closing years of the War of Independence. His interest in the Greeks was, as has been shown, no new sentiment. He had sympathised with their humiliation as early as 1801, when a boy-soldier in Abercromby's army, and his later command of Greek levies in the Ionian islands and the Peloponnesus had induced him not only to form a high opinion of their military capabilities, but also to cherish a sincere attachment to their character as displayed in many of his comrades in arms. On their side, the Greeks, who came in contact with him in the light infantry regiments which he had raised, were irresistibly drawn towards his frank and sympathetic nature, and would have done any service to merit his approbation and win his esteem. It was natural, in these mutual relations, that the War of Independence which broke out in 1821 should excite the deepest sympathy in one whose military and patriotic teaching had directly contributed to the insurrection. The only matter of surprise is that Church did not at once throw his lot in with his old officers and place his sword at the service of the Hellenic nation. The reasons are doubtless to be found in the weariness and disgust which attended his late experience in Palermo and Naples; in the reluctance of a British officer to risk his rank in his own service by volunteering in a cause which could not be countenanced by the Horse Guards; and in the natural desire, after so many years of exile and hard fighting, to settle awhile at home, among friends and in civilised society, and to take such pleasure and advancement as might be in store for him. Even so genuine an enthusiast as Sir Richard Church might well reflect before he sacrificed rank, fortune, ease, and prospects, in a cause which from the outset seemed absolutely desperate.

But as the war went on, and Greece grew weaker and weaker, he found his thoughts incessantly engrossed in her fate; and at length he could no longer resist the impulse to throw himself into the fight. In 1825 he was in frequent communication with Mr. Canning on the subject of the future of Greece, and soon afterwards the Greek deputies in London were soliciting his aid; but misunderstanding his character they coupled their invitation with inducements of high pay, and of course received an indignant refusal.[33] If he went at all, he said, it should be without the suspicion of self-interest or the hope of reward. In this frame of mind he wrote to his friend Blaquière, the well-known Philhellene:

15 Feb. 1826.

The cause is a sacred one, and Heaven will not abandon it in its hour of need. What do the Greeks wish me to do? Do they wish me to go? Do they wish that I shou'd not go? They must be explicit. I have no bargain to make with them, and this they clearly understand. I am ready to sacrifice everything to the cause, and this they know full well. . . . It is the feeling of my heart, and one that years has cherished. But I will not go as an Adventurer, no, never. What I have done for the Greeks, they themselves well know; if I have not done more, it is their fault and not mine. But this state of uncertainty must have an end—it kills me by inches. . . . Do the Greeks wish me to go, or not? It is for them to determine. If they think my services can be of use to their cause, let them say so, let them invite me. I ask no more, and I will with as little delay as possible add one more individual to the number of warriors fighting for Greece and freedom.

At length the official invitation was issued. Like the 'man of Macedonia,' the administrative commission of Greece sent forth the appeal: 'Come over and help us.' The formal request, written in Greek (with translations in French and English), is dated Napoli di Romania, 30 August, 1826 (O.S.):—

Excellency,—Your well-known military experience, joined to your noble sentiments and love of liberty, were calculated to draw towards you the attention of the Greek government, and the more so as it is sufficiently convinced of the warmth of your wishes for the success of the sacred struggle of Greece. The government has long desired and wished to see your excellency connected with the struggle of Greece for her holy rights; this would be considered a most fortunate event for our country, which would rightly expect from your talents great and pre-eminent ad-

---

[33] Finlay's imputation of 'mercenary' service (vi. 416, 417) is, like many other of his statements and inferences, the reverse of the truth.

vantages. The government, therefore, founding its hopes on your sincere love of Greece, and on your desire of real glory, invites your excellency expressly by these presents, and requests you to hasten to Greece, that you may take a principal part in her contest, and one conformable to your rank and character, and that you may employ your distinguished talents for the benefit of the Greek nation. The government confidently trusts that you will readily accept this invitation. It awaits with impatience your arrival, which it hopes will not be delayed, since the present critical position of Greece renders it most desirable.

Among the signatories to this document were the president, Andreas Zaemes, P. Mavromichales, A. Deliyannes, A. Monarchides, J. Vlachos, and other well-known names.

More impetuous was the personal letter which soon followed [34] from Church's former officer, and most typical of Klephts, Kolokotrones. Though parted for eight years, he tells the general—

> My soul has never been absent from you. . . . We, your old companions in arms . . . are fighting for our country—Greece, so dear to you!—that we may obtain our rights, as men and as a people, and our liberty. . . . How has your soul been able to remain from us? . . . I know your love for [Greece] increases in the same proportion as the respect and esteem of your old companions increases with regard to yourself. They all salute you most cordially, and hope even now soon to obtain your co-operation. Come! Come! and take up arms for Greece, or assist her with your talents, your virtues, and your abilities, that you may claim her eternal gratitude!

It is easy to imagine Church's reply to such an appeal. Yet he accepted in full cognisance of all the difficulties in his path. Personal sacrifices were nothing to him; even his recent marriage (in July) to a sister of Sir Robert Wilmot Horton (who was undersecretary for the colonies in Canning's ministry and afterwards governor of Ceylon) did not weigh in the balance against what he felt to be the call of duty. He knew the perilous uncertainty of the enterprise, and it is characteristic of his generous nature that, whilst freely devoting his all to the cause, he resolutely refused to have to answer to any friend for leading him into possible disaster. His letters to the officers who volunteered to accompany him are full of considerate balancing of risks. 'Count the cost' was his invariable advice. Nor was he blind to the jealousies and dissensions which paralysed the action of the Greeks, or to the lack of funds and provisions, which was enough to damp the ardour

---

[31] Napoli di Romania, $\frac{12}{24}$ September 1826.

of better troops than the undisciplined levies of Karaïskakes and Gordon.

In spite of all this he went, and November found him at Naples, successfully negotiating with his old ally Luigi De' Medicis for the opening of the ports of Apulia to Greek provision ships. He was at Leghorn in January 1827, and arrived in Argolis, on the eastern coast of the Peloponnesus, in March, a few days before Lord Cochrane's yacht made its appearance. The state of Greece was then well-nigh desperate. Ibrahim Pasha, son of the viceroy of Egypt, held the western side of the Peloponnesus with an army of nearly 50,000 men of all arms. His troops were strongly posted from Navarino to Patras, and he was receiving, so far, ample supplies from Alexandria. His personal ferocity, the raids of the Egyptians into central Peloponnesus, and the looting of helpless villages, had crushed the spirit of the inhabitants in many districts, insomuch that the Greeks on the west coast were beginning to submit to his yoke. Towards the eastern coast the people were still in arms— perhaps to the number of 10,000; the Maniats, the men of Sparta, of Monemvasia, and Corinth, were still able to harass the enemy; but it was hardly possible that they could repel him if he attempted to advance on Nauplia or Hydra. In continental Greece matters were even worse. Mesolonghi had fallen; the Turks he'd the northern shore of the gulf of Corinth with numerous garrisons, and kept their communications open for supplies and reinforcements with Larissa, Monastir, Arta, Prevesa, and Joannina; whilst Reshid Pasha Kiutahi dominated Attica with 40,000 men. Athens itself had fallen, but the Acropolis, garrisoned by over a thousand volunteers, and a small force of regulars under Colonel Fabvier, still withstood the pasha's siege. Between these two fires—Reshid in Attica and Ibrahim in the Peloponnesus—stood what remained of the Greek army. About 4,000 men under Karaïskakes were posted at Keratsina, near Port Phoron opposite Salamis, and Colonel Gordon had established a brigade on the heights of the Phalerum. Whatever good these small forces might have effected if properly employed was for the time frustrated by the dissensions of the Greek leaders. Two distinct assemblies, each styling itself the national assembly, were sitting, the one at Aegina, the other at Hermione (Kastri): the former advocated moderate measures, under the guidance of President Notaras; the latter was overruled by the turbulent spirit of Kolokotrones. Each rendered the other futile, and hampered the efforts of the provisional government, which was then led by the temperate counsels of President Zaemes.

Such was the depressing condition of the Greeks when Sir Richard Church landed near Kastri on 13 March, 1827. He was received with enthusiasm as an old friend by Kolokotrones, and with esteem by a staunch Philhellene, Captain Hamilton, of H.M.S. *Cambrian*, who described him as 'certainly a fine fellow, but a complete Irishman, with their great virtues and little faults.'[35] Karaïskakes sent him a warm letter of welcome, and begged the assembly to make him commander-in-chief. The government at Aegina, to whom he immediately reported himself, was equally sanguine as to the good influence he would bring to bear upon the distracted nation. Church took neither part in the dispute between the assemblies, but established himself at Poros to consider the situation. Here he received invitations from both sides to mediate between them; and so successful were his arguments that all differences were rapidly smoothed away, and a combined assembly, uniting all parties, was appointed to meet at Troezene (Damala).[36] This new body proceeded to the election of chief officers in April, and appointed Count John Capodistrias[37] president of Greece, Lord Cochrane high admiral, and Sir R. Church archistrategos or commander-in-chief of the land forces.[38] He took the oaths on sword and book, 15 April.

The new generalissimo's first anxiety was of course to relieve the Acropolis of Athens, but without men, money, ammunition, or food, how was this to be done? Church's opinion was strongly in favour of a diversion in continental Greece, which, by raising the Albanians, Epirots, Akarnanians, and others, should draw off the attention of the besiegers from the Acropolis; but he was fully aware of the hazards of this plan. There was a pressing want of

---

[35] Hamilton to Stratford Canning, Poros, 19 April, 1827.

[36] A letter from Kolokotrones to Church, 24 March (5 April), distinctly ascribes this happy result to Sir Richard's mediation, and the same conviction is stated by Capt. Fallon, A.D.C. (letter to Sir R. Wilmot Horton, 14 Nov. 1828), who adds: 'No other person could have effected the herculean task of accommodating and reconciling hitherto inimical parties.' Kolokotrones concluded his letter with the deprecatory sentence: οἱ Ἕλληνες ἦναι ἀκόμη ἔθνος νήπιον, καὶ νηπιώδη τὰ Ἑλληνικά, ὅθεν μὴ δυσαρεστῆσθε οὕτως εὐκόλως δ' αὐτά.

[37] Finlay regards this appointment as made in opposition to the two Cannings vi. 421 and note): the fact is that Sir Stratford Canning was consulted and approved it (*Life of Sir Stratford Canning*, i. 443).

[38] The appointment was not solicited (or 'obtained,' in Finlay's suggestive word), but freely offered.

money and transports, the northern Greeks might not rise at his
summons, the Turkish garrisons on the gulf of Corinth were
numerous, and meanwhile the Acropolis might fall. Another plan
he recommended was an expedition to Negropont, to cut off the
Turkish supplies and communications. The council of war did not
support either project.[39] Lord Cochrane had from the outset
strenuously insisted on an immediate advance on Athens, in order
at all costs to bring out the garrison; but this proposal was
equally combated by the Greek generals, and could not prudently
be attempted unless a strong contingent were sent to reinforce the
army in Attica. Such a force could only be drawn from the
Peloponnesus, which would consequently be exposed to imminent
danger from Ibrahim's army; and every position that could be
maintained between the forces of Ibrahim and Reshid naturally
lessened the serious risk of a junction being effected between the
Turks and the Egyptians.

Nevertheless, it was resolved that Karaïskakes' army at Ports
Phoron and Phalerum must be reinforced, whatever might subsequently be decided with regard to an immediate advance upon
Athens. In three days Church had made his preparations for
transporting 4,500 men from the eastern coasts of the Peloponnesus
to Attica; and on 18 April he proceeded on Cochrane's schooner to
the port of the Phalerum to reconnoitre the positions of the two
armies. Sailing along the coast, the Turks' principal batteries on
the Philopappus (near the Museum) could be seen shelling the
Acropolis; they held most of the plain beneath, were strongly
posted in the great olive wood, and had a series of redoubts opposite
the Greek camp at Phoron, which they cut off from the force on
the Phalerum by retaining a garrison at the monastery of St.
Spiridion on the neck of land between the Peiraeus and the port of
Munychia. The armies were thus curiously intersected, and
Turkish forces separated the three Greek divisions in a menacing
manner.[40] The chief hope lay in the free communication which
existed between the two camps on the coast and the fleet under
Lord Cochrane in the Peiraeus.

On the 19th Church went ashore at Port Phoron ('Harbour of
Thieves' once, and perhaps not yet quite purified), under a some-

---

[39] 'Church's plan for taking possession of all the posts and passes in rear of
Athens, for the purpose of cutting off the Turkish supplies, was strongly combated'
(Capt. Fallon's *Diary*).

[40] Capt. Fallon's *Diary*, 18 April 1827.

what embarrassing salute of *ball* cartridges, and was received by Karaïskakes in great state, in spite of the misery of his camp, where there was no bread, hardly any meat, no stores, and only fifty-three boxes of cartridges.

The next few days were spent in bringing over the reinforcements to the Phalerum, 25 April; in moving Karaïskakes, after much remonstrance, from Phoron to a better position on the Peiraeus 26 April; in reconnoitring the enemy's outposts, and taking a few of the nearest *tambours* or breastworks.

The small skirmishes of the week may be passed over; but a word must be said of the slaughter of the majority (170) of the garrison of St. Spiridion, after their surrender on terms of safe conduct on 28 April. Church felt the dishonour so keenly that he resigned his command, and for a day nothing could appease his indignation; but as the evidence came before him in detail, he convinced himself that the massacre of the Turks was the result of an accidental quarrel, and was not premeditated; and that Karaïskakes and Zavellas, who commanded the Greek escort, believed they had taken every precaution against an outbreak of illwill, and when the disturbance began used their utmost endeavours (according to their own statements) at some personal risk to quell it and save the garrison. Church himself could in no way be held responsible, since he was waiting at his head-quarters at the old arsenal of the Peiraeus for Karaïskakes to return and report the result of his mission to the monastery, and had no suspicion that the Greek general would march the garrison out then and there; and when the march began, there was of course no time to do anything but look on in helpless horror from the opposite shore.

Meanwhile circumstances were driving the general more and more irresistibly towards the premature advance which he so much deprecated. Lord Cochrane had urgently pressed this course from the first, and a despatch from the garrison at the Acropolis left little room for any alternative. In this despatch (April $\frac{14}{23}$), after reproaching the Greek commanders with want of good faith in not sooner coming to their rescue, the leaders of the garrison concluded:

> This is our last letter; we will wait five days longer, and we can hold out no more. . . . Our nature is like that of all men; we can suffer no more than others. We are neither angels nor workers of miracles to raise the dead or do impossible things. If any evil should happen, we are not to blame, nor has God to condemn us in anything.

The document was signed by seven 'patriots' and confirmed by Colonel Fabvier. It was afterwards proved that these statements were false:[41] that there were food and powder enough to last for months; but this could not of course be known at the time to either Church or Cochrane, though the Greek generals evidently had their suspicions. The admiral naturally redoubled his endeavours in favour of an immediate march to save the beleaguered garrison. His letters from the arrival of this despatch to the ill-fated battle of 6 May display his well-known impetuosity; his utter (and not unwarranted) distrust of the Greek leaders, whom he could neither understand nor manage; and his determination to force an action at any cost. On 23 April he wrote to Church:

> 'People on the Phalere *will not* advance into the centre of the plain, being, as they are, *unbelievers* in the advance of the army on Athens.' On the 24th: 'Forty-eight hours, and the question of relieving Athens is at a close. I have told Kariaskaky [sic] what I think of the state of affairs, and I have made up my mind to act accordingly—taking upon me all the responsibility of not looking longer on at insignificant tambour disputes, whilst it seems resolved by the Greeks themselves not to march to the relief of Athens.'

For the next few days his lordship found a safety-valve for his zeal in forcing the Greeks to remove their camp, as has been stated, from Phoron to the Peiraeus, and then in razing the monastery of St. Spiridion; but as soon as these matters were arranged he returned to the attack (28 April):

> 'Pray let me know if the army *will* or *will not* advance, and if that advance will take place before to-morrow evening.' 29th: 'A direct march on Athens and return by another road is the only means of averting total destruction to the garrison and to Greece.'

At 8 on the following evening, 30 April, the admiral despatched the following ultimatum to the commander-in-chief: '*I leave this to-morrow:*— 1st, *if the army will not march, on a false attack being made elsewhere by the squadron; 2ndly, if 2,000 men, in lieu thereof, do not embark and proceed direct to Athens; 3rdly, if no other reasonable plan is to be adopted and to be put in execution before the morning of 2 May. And this I shall do as certainly as I live to put my determination in execution.*'

The last extract is here printed in italics, because so extraordi-

---

[41] This is fully confirmed by Finlay (vi. 409, 432), who ascribes the disasters at Athens largely to Fabvier's unscrupulous resolution to get out of the Acropolis after Church's appointment to the command-in-chief.

nary an interference of an admiral in military strategy ought to be signalised, and also because the passionate gallantry which dictated it was the main cause of the disaster that befell the Greeks a week later. Church was no coward, nor no Fabius neither, but he saw the hopelessness of the hasty admiral's tactics, and, supported by all the Greek commanders, he tried to wait for his opportunity, instead of forcing fortune. But Cochrane was resolute; let them act, he said, or off he would instantly sail [42] and leave the whole force of nearly 10,000 men to starve or be massacred; and thus it happened that at two councils of war, held in the early days of May, the fatal forward movement was planned and agreed to. It was against Church's judgment; but even the Greek generals had given in, and as they were to arrange the details the archistrategos considered himself bound to stand aside.

At this juncture Karaïskakes was killed in a skirmish (4 May), and this threw a new responsibility upon the chief. So long as this officer lived, Church had been considerately deferent to his views and susceptibilities, and had done his utmost to conciliate a man naturally jealous and difficult to manage. He had left him this rank as commander-in-chief in Attica; and so great was his desire for unity and conciliation, that the Greek soldier, in consideration of his undoubted services and military talents, had far more than his due weight in the councils of war. It was to this that Lord Cochrane referred when he wrote to Church (30 April), 'Nothing will be done by the army, so long as Kariaskaki commands it *in reality.*' There can be little doubt that part, at least, of the ill success of the war in Attica was due to the generalissimo's exaggerated deference to Karaïskakes. Divided commands seldom succeed; and with Karaïskakes arguing one way, and Cochrane another, it must have appeared obvious to every spectator that the Greeks needed *one* head, and that head ashore. Church had an opportunity of assuming the complete and direct command after the massacre of the garrison of St. Spiridion, which afforded an ample pretext for depriving Karaïskakes of any post requiring caution and forethought; but his kindly nature restrained him. Now that the Greek general was dead, he at length took the actual command; but it was too late to rouse a new spirit in the army,

---

[42] *Diary* of C. Fallon, A.D.C., 6 May. Tricoupi, iv. 66, signalises the arrogance with which Cochrane forced his rash scheme upon the council, and his habitual rejoinder to every argument, 'that he would take off ships and money and leave Greece to perish.'

as he might have done had he taken his rightful place from the beginning. It needed every prompting of enthusiastic patriotism to induce a few thousand ill-fed and worse-armed Greeks to march against ten times their number of Turks; yet this was what had to be done, in cold blood, and without a spark of enthusiasm, three days later.

On the day after the death of Karaïskakes, preparations were pressed forward for the attack on the rear of the besiegers, advancing from the south, in accordance with Lord Cochrane's plan. The choice of the ground and the disposition of the troops were entirely in the hands of the Greek commanders, who said that they were the best judges of the country and position, and who declined to go into action on any other terms. Every detail had previously been drawn up by Karaïskakes and his colleagues at two councils of war. At sunset on 5 May, the embarkation began, but it was not till 3 in the morning that the landing on the coast beyond Cape Kolias, famous for the wrecking of the Persian fleet after Salamis, could be commenced, and daylight overtook them before the expedition of 3,000 infantry (with no cavalry, and only two or three small mountain guns) was ashore. As the sun rose, Captain Fallon went forward and reconnoitred the position. He found the first line of the Greeks pushed forward in the plain, to within about a mile of Athens; the reserves, about three-quarters of a mile to the rear; and between them, a line of badly connected *tambours*.[43] Already he could perceive the Turkish cavalry massing in the distance.

It was clear that as a surprise—a rush by night to the relief of the Acropolis—the expedition was already a failure. Even if there had been the least chance of success so near daybreak, that chance had been thrown away and the brief moments wasted in throwing up ineffectual earthworks, instead of pressing forward at all hazards. What remained to be done did not rest with General Church; it had been pre-arranged by the council of war under the direction of Karaïskakes. The Greeks were to take to the rocky ground to the south and south-west of the Acropolis, and hold the position till night, when they and the 7,000 troops left on the Phalerum, and the 1,300 men in the Acropolis (who had been duly informed of the movement), would make a simultaneous desperate onslaught upon the Turks from all sides. In accordance with these orders, the Greeks strengthened their works (if slight mounds, thrown up with a totally inadequate supply of engineering tools,

---

[43] *Diary*, 6 May. See the accompanying Plan, drawn at the time by an eyewitness.

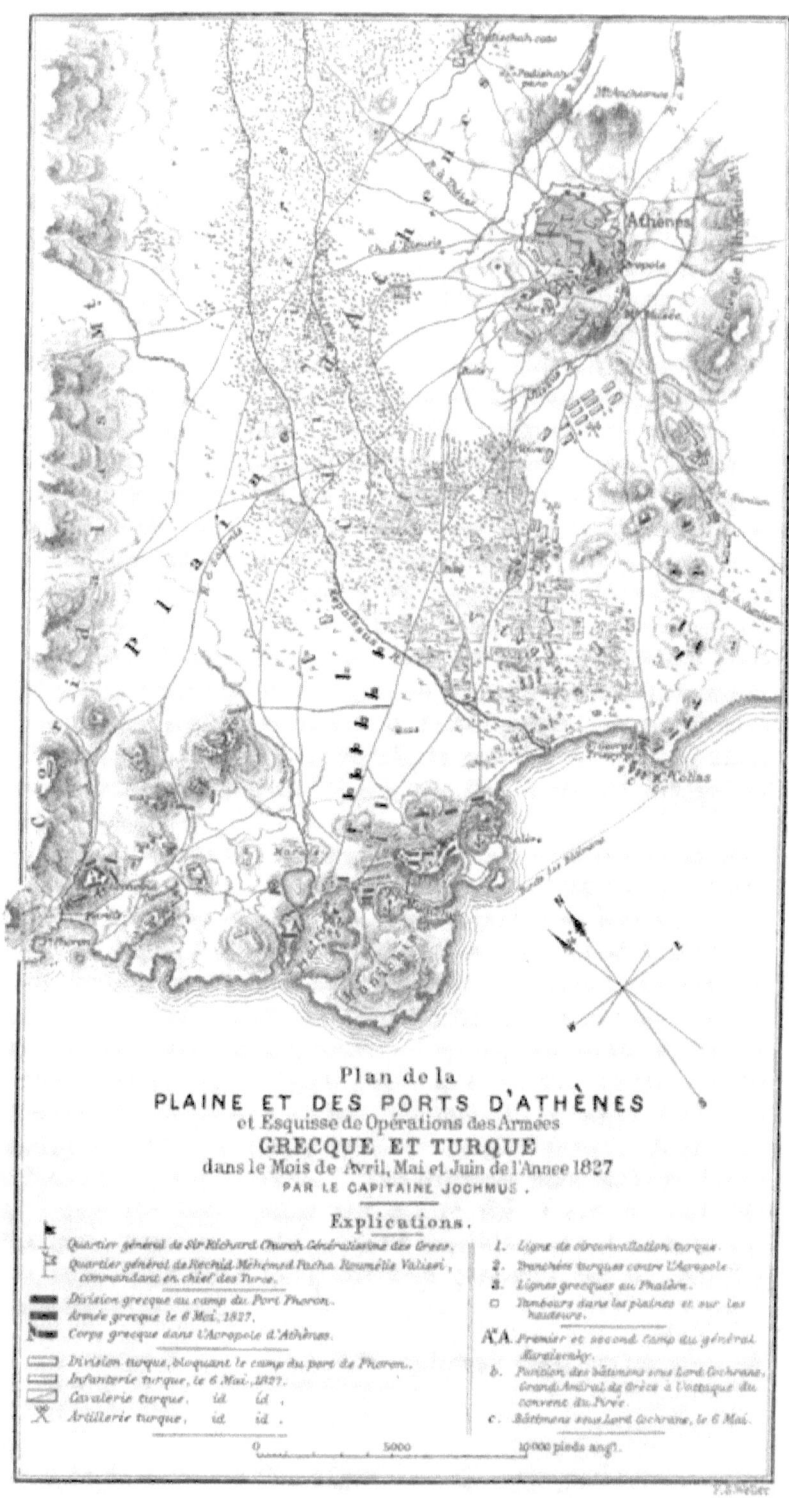

Plan de la
PLAINE ET DES PORTS D'ATHÈNES
et Esquisse de Opérations des Armées
GRECQUE ET TURQUE
dans le Mois de Avril, Mai et Juin de l'Année 1827
PAR LE CAPITAINE JOCHMUS.

deserve the name) to some extent, but do not appear to have taken up higher ground; they remained in the same positions till past noon. All this time the Turkish cavalry was gathering in force, and their infantry was also on the march. Church quickly saw that it was hopeless to try to hold his ground unaided, and he sent repeated orders [44] to General Zavellas, who was in command of the 7,000 men left at the Phalerum, to advance to the attack from the other side. This was evidently what the Turkish general expected: he would not have spared Church's exposed and inadequate force of 3,000 men so long unless he had regarded their movement as a feint to mask a general action. But Zavellas was deaf to the requests of the commander-in-chief, and blind to the necessities of the situation. No movement was made from the Phalerum, and the Turks advanced with increased confidence upon the Greek positions on the Museum hill within two hours after noon. The patriots, with few exceptions, made no manner of stand: General Vasso was the first to take to his heels, and Costa Botzaris seems to have been little bolder; [45] some companies ran without firing, others fired wildly and then ran, others got rid of their ammunition safely before the enemy had come within double musket range; all save a few Suliots were speedily in full flight, and two out of every three were overtaken and slain. Such was the 'battle of Athens' of 6 May, 1827.

Church had viewed the scene, and given such orders as were possible, from a small redoubt at the church of St. George of the Tris Pyrgi near the shore. Cochrane stayed there with him until all was over, and the flight of the Greeks summoned him to his ships to assist and protect the embarkation. At last the generalissimo was forced to leave too; those of his troops who had escaped the scimetar were on the beach or among the rocks, where the Turks could not easily reach them, and the lives of the general staff were in imminent peril from the presence of bodies of Turkish cavalry in close proximity to their slender shelter. There was nothing for it but to retire. The fugitives were skilfully taken on board the ships under the fire of the Turks without the loss of a single man; the dejected expedition sailed back to the Phalerum; and here ended the first period of Sir R. Church's campaign in Greece.

[44] No mention is made of these orders in Finlay's history, but Tricoupi, iv. 66, comments on Zavellas's gross insubordination.

[45] Fallon's *Diary*.

So far it had been remarkable chiefly for a great disaster. Yet on Church's behalf it may fairly be urged that what success there was, was his doing, and what failure there was cannot be set down to his discredit. He had succeeded in uniting the rival parties in Greece; he had strengthened the army in Attica; and after the defeat of 6 May he had brought off the remainder of his troops without loss under the enemy's fire.[46]

The battle of Athens was not of his choosing, nor were the dispositions of the troops his: the battle was forced on by Cochrane, and the dispositions were arranged by Karaïskakes, in the council of war. The only criticism that can fairly be put upon General Church is that under the conditions he should not have accepted the command. He should have been chief in action as well as in name, or never chief at all. The divided power, the independence of Karaïskakes (which formed a precedent for Zavellas's subsequent disobedience of orders), the interference of the high admiral— these were causes enough to paralyse the energies of any man; and Church, for his own name's sake, ought never to have exposed himself to the trial. But the general was one of those men who do not think of themselves, but of a great cause. To him, the liberation of Greece was a holy war, and he felt that to withdraw from it, even temporarily and under extreme provocation, might be doing an injury hard to be endured in that time of disaster and despair. So he had held on, despite the opposition and foolhardy policy of others, the blame of which would surely fall upon himself, and so he would continue to hold on for the sake of Greece.

It was after the disastrous battle of Athens that Church's remarkable qualities as a leader of undisciplined troops came into full play.[47] So far he had felt himself compelled for the general good to take almost a secondary part, while Cochrane and Karaïskakes practically guided the councils of war. But now the jealous Greek commander was dead, and the admiral had sailed away to concentrate

---

[46] This account of Church's conduct of the war in Attica is derived from his own narrative and letters, and from his A.D.C., Fallon's *Diary*. It differs seriously from Finlay's version, which can hardly be acquitted of the charge of unfairness.

[47] The authorities for this period of General Church's career are too numerous to be as a rule individually cited. They consist in a voluminous correspondence with the principal leaders in Greece at the time, besides the Philhellene Committees outside Greece; in Church's own memoirs and narratives; and in various letters and reports from most of the chief actors in the revolutionary movement. A special debt of gratitude must be acknowledged to Canon Church's notes and analysis of correspondence, and to his article 'The Greek Frontier, how it was won in 1829,' in the *New Quarterly Magazine*, July 1879.

his ships, in view of a possible approach of the Turkish fleet, leaving Church to do the best he could to 'prevail on the dastardly gang to hold the Phalerum,' or if not, to 'get away from the scene of their disgrace.' This was the usual tone of impatient Philhellenes, who tried to work miracles with a handful of disorganised volunteers, and then reviled them because the miracles were not worked. Such was not Church's way. He had every cause to be disheartened by his first few weeks' experience, but he was not the man to lose courage at the first reverse, or to despair of the cause to which he was pledged because the instruments he had to use were imperfect. The bad workman proverbially complains of his tools: Church preferred to make the best of them; and if it cannot be averred that he ever produced a perfect edge, at least no one but him succeeded in keeping them from rusting altogether.

After the retreat on 6 May, a scene of panic and despair prevailed throughout the camp, and taxed to the utmost the general's powers of persuasion and control. Many of the Peloponnesians deserted; the rest could not be induced at first to touch a spade or a musket; and the fleet had sailed away, leaving hardly more than 3,000 disheartened half-starved Greeks exposed to the inclemency of the elements (for they had no tents on the heights of the Phalerum), and to the assaults of at least 30,000 Turks, who could probably drive them bodily into the sea at any moment. Amid the murmurs of the chiefs and the open rebellion of the men, the general alone retained his coolness and cheerful confidence. He possessed no military authority over troops who were mere volunteers, neither enrolled nor regularly paid by the government, and scarcely even fed; he had to trust only to his personal ascendency and the respect and enthusiasm which his well-known courage, his devotion to Greece, and his invincible patience and kindliness inspired in his followers. So great, however, was this influence, that he contrived to keep his dejected little army in position on the Phalerum (or Munychia) for three weeks, without pay or adequate provisions, and in presence of an overwhelming force of the enemy; and at last he only drew off his men because they were running short of water, and were doing no real good in their cramped situation.

When he had resolved to make a move, he took a farewell survey of the scene.

Early on the morning of 27 May [to quote his own narrative], the general-in-chief walked round the entrenchments of the Phalerum, and when on the summit of this renowned hill, once an impregnable fortress, the glorious surrounding scenery impressed his mind with the most powerful sensations: Athens on one side, closely blockaded by a barbarous multitude incessantly occupied in discharging ponderous volleys of heavy artillery against the Acropolis, shells bursting over the Parthenon; in front of the Phalerum the long line of the Turkish camp stretching from the sea near Cape Kolias to the Peiraeus, forming almost a semicircle, in order the better to envelop the few Greek troops posted in their front; the immense number of standards and of tents of all colours, the plain covered with horses, mules, camels, and sheep; on the other side, the island of Salamis, always ready to receive the Greeks when driven out of Attica; further off the mighty Geraneion and Mount Oenion, the bulwarks of Peloponnesus; and Aegina directly in front, whence came Aristides to aid his immortal rival in their efforts for the salvation of their country on the awful night preceding the battle of Salamis.

The Greeks who accompanied their general were evidently impressed with the scene and its associations, and it was with a sore sense of the contrast between the past and the present that they retraced their steps, and prepared to leave the historic soil of Attica.

On the same night all was in readiness, and at daybreak on the 28th the embarkation was in rapid progress. By the time the Turks, who had early become aware of the movement, were on the heights of the Phalerum, three-fourths of the Greeks were on board the Ipsariot flotilla, which Church had managed to procure from Aegina; and so skilfully had all the arrangements been planned, and so well directed was the covering fire of the Greeks among the rocks, that the whole army was safely embarked without the loss of a single man, in spite of the efforts of a strong and exasperated force of the enemy under Reshid Pasha in person. The troops were landed at Salamis, and Church established his head-quarters at Aegina.

One of his aides-de-camp, who had been with him throughout the campaign, wrote not long afterwards [48] that

considering the measures he has adopted, the incredible difficulties he has had to overcome, particularly in the total want of pay and provisions for his troops, he has effected more than any other person could have done under similar circumstances, through the extraordinary firmness of character he possesses, and the popular feeling, particularly of the army, in his favour; which has enabled him to perform the almost incredible task of keeping an armed force together without pay or subsistence.

[48] C. Fallon, A.D.C., to Rt. Hon. R. Wilmot Horton, Rome, 14 Nov. 1828.

CHAPTER VIII.

THE CAMPAIGN IN WESTERN GREECE.

1827–1829.

DURING the next few months matters remained very much *in statu quo*. The Turks were to a great extent paralysed by the action of the allies. England, France, and Russia signed the Treaty of London for the pacification of Greece, 6 July, and sent their fleets to the Levant to put pressure upon the Turks and Egyptians. Further, they declared an armistice to exist between the belligerents, which the Greeks accepted and the Turks refused. Nevertheless, when Captain Hastings, acting for the Greeks, destroyed a Turkish flotilla at Salona, it was not regarded as a breach of the armistice which the Greeks had accepted; but when Ibrahim Pasha, who had rejected it, sent a squadron to the gulf of Corinth to punish Hastings, it was turned back by the allies: such were the principles of this singular neutrality. Meanwhile, on shore both sides were inactive. Ibrahim took a few forts, but struck no decisive blow; and the Greeks, without money, and short of ammunition and food, either tendered a temporary submission, or gathered in disorderly bands under their favourite chiefs, and indulged in local depredations for their private behoof. There was no unity, no organisation, and little public spirit. The executive government was weak and divided; the treasury was empty. The better sort of patriots awaited anxiously the long-delayed arrival of the new president, Count John Capodistrias.

Under such circumstances Church, with all his energy and influence, could effect little to good purpose. He had not, however, been idle. Before leaving Attica he had taken three measures, each of which showed remarkable foresight and was fraught with important issues. The first was the establishment of a Greek camp at the Great Derven on Mount Geraneion, which effectually prevented the entrance of Reshid Pasha's army into the Peloponnesus and his junction with Ibrahim after the surrender of the Acropolis on 5 June. The second was the despatch of most of his Peloponnesian volunteers back to their homes, where they were instructed to encourage their neighbours, and prepare for a general rising. The third was the result of a long-considered plan. From the beginning, as has been seen, Church had anxiously debated where he could best create a diversion to draw off the Turks from Attica. Two ideas occurred to him: one was a descent upon eastern Greece and Negropont, with the view to attacking Reshid in the rear, and cutting off his supplies both by sea and land; the other was a landing in Akarnania, where the western provinces could be raised, the Albanians' disaffection to the Turks fomented into an alliance with the Greeks, and the Ottoman garrisons starved into surrender. Neither of these plans was approved at first by the Greek government, and it may be doubted whether in the spring of 1827 transports or money could have been provided for any considerable expedition, or whether political events had yet created a favourable opportunity for such movements as Church contemplated. Still, he never lost sight of his design, and when he began to take steps for abandoning the position on the Phalerum one of his first proceedings was to prepare for a descent upon western Greece by sending a few men to stir up the people of Akarnania.

The result of this small mission was the seizure by Demozelio of an island in the lake of Lessini, near the Achelous (Aspropotamos), which he defended so well (partly with guns which had belonged to Byron and been buried on the island) that six months later Church found him in full possession, despite a long Turkish blockade; and the same creditable defence was maintained by Demetrius Makri at the neighbouring Mount Zygos. Such was the insignificant beginning of a movement which led to the liberation of western Greece and the eventual enlargement of the boundaries of the emancipated kingdom.

This first small step could not be immediately followed up. Church's task after his retreat from Attica was diplomatic rather than military: he had to reconcile as best he could rival chiefs, inspire a better and more disinterested public spirit, and try every resource for the replenishment of the treasury and the commissariat. It was uphill work enough, in the divided state of parties and the jealous clan-spirit of the insubordinate military chiefs; but his tact and conciliatory manner, his genial treatment of his old followers—rather as a father over a pack of unruly children than as a commanding officer—his strong moral influence, probably effected all that was possible under the circumstances. It may be questioned whether he made his authority sufficiently feared; but he certainly gained the love and respect of his men, and retained their devotion when all other commanders despaired of keeping any force together. To him was chiefly due the maintenance of the important camp at Mount Geraneion and the support of the garrisons at Acrocorinthus, Salamis, Megara, and elsewhere. Even with all his efforts a steady advance of Turks and Egyptians must infallibly have overwhelmed the Greeks; and to their inactivity and the English policy which culminated in the battle of Navarino, Greece owed her freedom.

The plan of an expedition to eastern Greece and the Negropont was again proposed in July, but fell through for want of money and provisions. The descent upon Akarnania remained to be tried. The Turks and Egyptians were so busy in devastating Attica and the Peloponnesus that their regular troops had almost deserted western continental Greece; and Cochrane told Church in August (with his usual reckless exaggeration) that the whole country between Prevesa and Mesolonghi was up in arms, and added, 'Were you present, the Turks would soon be driven from all their possessions on the northern shore of the gulf of Corinth.' The admiral accordingly urged Church to carry out 'your first plan;' forgetting doubtless how strenuously he had opposed that plan at the outset. In the existing state of affairs, political, financial, and military, it was impossible to muster an army for western Greece at a week's notice; but throughout the autumn measures were carefully matured with a view to that expedition. Provision had first to be made for the defence of the Greek positions in the Peloponnesus; the jealousies of the military leaders had to be appeased; προσκυνούμενοι, or Greeks who had paid forced submission to the enemy, had if possible to be drawn over to the patriotic side and protected from the revenge of the Egyptians and the resentment of stronger-minded patriots; the universal lust of pillage had to be mitigated; and in all these matters Church, as commander-in-chief, was the prime arbiter and referee. So distressing to his upright nature were the petty squabbles and dishonesties of the chiefs, that he declared bitterly that he would rather meet a column of Turks than a petition of contumacious Greeks. At last the news of the battle of Navarino (20 Oct.) brought matters to a crisis. The disaster to the Turks, and the obvious sympathy of the great powers with the Greeks, revived the national spirit in all parts of Hellas. Now, said Cochrane, was the moment to act; and his words found a welcoming echo in the heart of General Church. He at once took measures for the long-desired expedition; wrote ($\frac{3}{15}$ Nov.) to Captain Hastings to bring his flotilla out of the gulf of Corinth to Cape Papas, at the extreme west of Achaia, and prepare to transport a force across the gulf of Lepanto to Akarnania. He could not fix a day for the

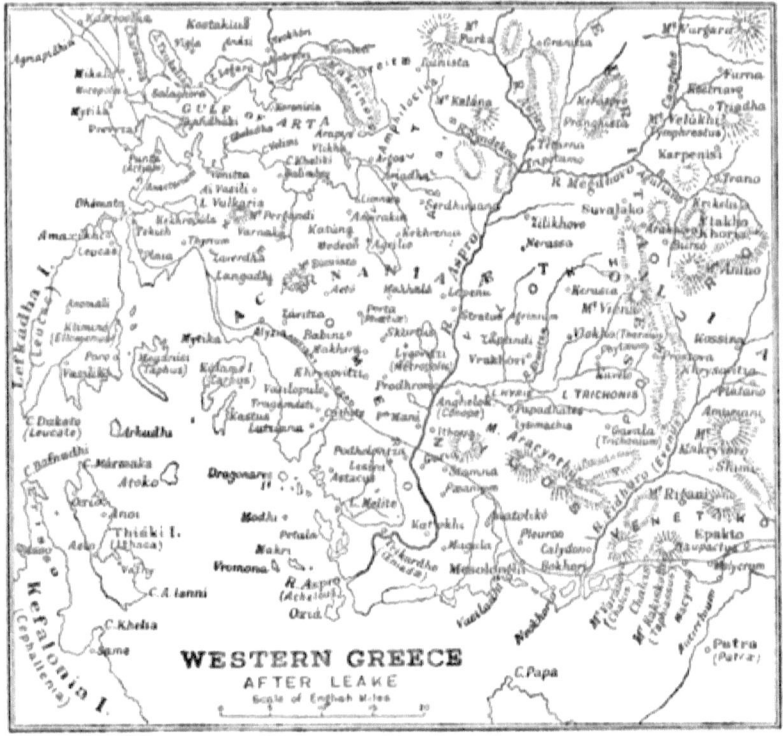

rendezvous,[49] he said, because a large force of the enemy's cavalry was reported to command the plains of Elis, but he would start immediately. Delayed by the necessity of manœuvring to avoid the cavalry, by want of money and ammunition, and by heavy rains, he did not reach Cape Papas till 28 Nov. The march across, through the mountains of Achaia, had been difficult and perilous, and the ravines of Mount Olonos had become almost impassable

[49] Finlay's implied reproach (vii. 22) for delay is vitiated by Church's having forewarned Hastings of his inability to fix a date for their meeting.

with their swollen torrents. Food was often hard to procure, for
the wretched villagers knew not at first which was their worse
enemy, the Egyptians or the *palikari*, and it needed all Church's
patience and kindness to convince them of his goodwill. On the
26th he arrived at the convent of Philokali, overlooking the plain of
the Kamenitza, and here he dismissed the Peloponnesians, whom
(for want of necessary supplies) he did not intend to take over with
him, to the number of 4,000 or 5,000, and keeping only the 1,200
Rumeliots led by Botzaris he marched across the Elian plain,
through heavy swamps in which the men sank almost to their
shoulders, to Cape Papas at the very moment when Ahmed Pasha
was bringing his cavalry over the Kamenitza.

Then [on 29 Nov.] with a force which he had gradually sifted, like
Gideon's host, till he retained with him only 1,000 men, the number which
Hastings undertook to carry across, he made a landing at Dragomestre
[Astakos] on the Akarnanian coast in two divisions of 500 men, [the second
crossing on 6 Dec.] His purpose was to raise the country on both sides
of the Aspropotamos, and to occupy the gulf of Arta and the range of
Makrinoros, certain that by so doing he should cut the communication
with Mesolonghi and the gulf of Lepanto, and force the garrisons to surrender. And, beyond that, he hoped, if sufficiently supported, to throw a
force upon the northern coast of Epirus, to distract the attention of the
Turks at Joannina by giving encouragement to the disaffected northern
Albanians, or at least to raise the districts of Parga, Souli, and Arta,
and to threaten Prevesa by land, while a naval force co-operated in the
attack.[50]

At this time the Turks were undisputed masters of continental
Greece. Cochrane's enthusiastic report of the rising of the whole
western country was not confirmed by Church's personal observation. On the contrary, most of the Greek chiefs who had submitted
to the Turks after the fall of Mesolonghi still remained in their
service, and in many cases their patriotism was narrowed to a
cautious balancing of the chances of success : they would join the
winning side, but were not disposed to espouse the national cause
hastily, lest worse evils should befall them even than those they
had already suffered. The chances of success seemed very small
for the little force at Dragomestre. Operating from Joannina,
Arta, and Prevesa, the Turks held a chain of fortified posts—whether
loopholed khans, walled monasteries, or mere villages and breast-

---

[50] C. M. Church, *New Quarterly Review*, July 1879, pp. 9, 10. The accompanying map will illustrate the positions occupied by the Greeks.

works commanding the mountain tracks—all the way from their garrisons at Mesolonghi and Anatolico on the gulf of Lepanto to the forts of Vonitza and Kervasara on the gulf of Arta, and then across the Makrinoros range to Kombotti and Prevesa. Had they attacked Church's small force at once, there could hardly have been a doubt of their success. But their regular troops were considerably diminished, probably in view of the coming war with Russia, and the rivalries of their chief commanders destroyed all unity of action. Church was accordingly allowed to land unopposed, and once established on shore it did not take him long to convert Dragomestre into a sort of humble Torres Vedras—a base of operations against the Turks in western Greece. In this he was favoured by the natural position of the place. The land approach, across mountain passes, marshes, and dense forests, offered every obstacle to an enemy; the rocky bays and inlets of the coast presented dangers to a naval attack; and the Paleo Castro and monastery of St. Elia possessed the elements of strong forts. Church lost no time in improving these advantages. He quickly constructed breastworks and redoubts of the ordinary native sort (loopholed walls of loose stone, surrounded by abattis of trees and brushwood), strengthened the monastery and castro, and formed an entrenched camp, armed with a few guns. He wrote to the government (14 Dec.):

We have worked incessantly in throwing up field-works and in strengthening our position, as far as is in our power to do so. I have bought some prize guns—six, nine, and twelve pounders,—iron guns, from Captain Hastings, with which it is my intention to arm some excellent boats acting with the army under brave and patriotic captains and crews. It is my intention, as far as it is in my power, to make this place, Dragomestre, a *base d'opérations* for western Greece, from whence to proceed, with God's aid, to the recovery of the whole of this beautiful province from the Turkish domination. This must be effected by the patriotic and energetic co-operation with me of its warlike Greek population, by my having a flotilla in the gulf of Arta, and by my being provided with provisions.

Having made Dragomestre as safe as he could, Church began to reconnoitre the country, intercept Turkish convoys and messengers (sometimes with striking success), and raise the Greek chiefs of the neighbourhood. Foremost of all came in the valiant Demozelio, who had held the island of Lessini unsupported for six months, but was now relieved by the retreat of the blockading

Turks upon the news of Church's landing. To induce the other chiefs to join demanded tact and resolution. They must be taught that this new expedition was no filibustering raid, and therefore the camp must be kept in order and no depredations permitted. They must be convinced that the expedition was destined to triumph, and therefore no chance must be given to the Turks of the smallest success. Fortunately for these objects, the troops behaved well, and the Turks retired instead of advancing. The consequence was the speedy adhesion of various Greek chieftains who had not hitherto ventured to throw off their Turkish yoke, or who had hidden themselves in the mountains in despair of ever again striking a blow for independence.

Staïcos raised the Greek standard on his castled crag of Vlochos (Thermos), the Aetolian capital, which commanded the plains of Vrachori, and cut off convoys and detachments passing to and from Mesolonghi. Makres of Apokoros and Makriyannes of Zygos brought up their men to join Staïcos. Zonga, a large sheepmaster, whose possessions lay round Vonitza and the peninsula of Actium, came in with 500 followers. Varnakiottes, the chief man of Xeromeros, the western district of Akarnania, led 300 of his men by night through the Turkish position, and joined the camp [now formed by Church] at Mitika [on the north-west coast, near the gulf of Arta]. Andreas Iskos, chief of Valtos, who held the passes of Makrinoros, made promises of coming over as soon as the Greek force was strong enough to make it safe for him to leave the Turks.[51]

Church had now something like 3,000 men under his command, not indeed regular soldiers, but still hardy mountaineers who could be employed with effect in a guerilla warfare such as was in contemplation. 'It is an army of volunteers,' he wrote to the president, 18 Feb., 'and every man serves under the chief he likes best, being neither enlisted, enrolled, nor subject to articles of war, nor has the general legal right to command or punish; so it must be while they are not regularly paid, fed, nor clothed by the government—such is the nature of the army. I have had to struggle with the Turks for the liberation of Greece, and the difficulties I have had to encounter are incredible; but I must say in justice to those brave men, that I have rarely had to find fault with them, and they have followed me under the most trying circumstances.' A second force of 1,200 men had also under his instructions effected a landing within the gulf of Lepanto, opposite the little island of Trisognia.[52] The main difficulty was to provision the troops. The

[51] C. M. Church, l.c. 10.   [52] Sir R. Church to Captain Hastings, 28 Dec. 1827

government had little money, or at all events sent little; the country around Dragomestre could not supply the wants of the army and of the numerous families who took refuge under Church's protection ; and for the pay of the troops recourse was had to the Philhellenic commission at Corfu, whose funds, however, were much smaller than rumour asserted. It may be stated, once for all, that from the beginning to the end of the campaign Church's army was never adequately provisioned or paid; that the money, clothes, tents, supplies, and reinforcements repeatedly promised by the government of Aegina, in response to the general's urgent remonstrances, never arrived, or only came in miserable driblets; and that again and again the whole expedition was threatened with total collapse in consequence of the negligence and incapacity of the central authorities. These charges could be proved in all their miserable details, were the proof worth the space.[53]

In spite of these hindrances, Church resolved on a forward movement. And here he again encountered the vexation of a divided command. His plan of seizing the gulf of Arta and the Makrinoros required naval co-operation.[54] Captain Hastings, however, had other views for his flotilla—he took possession[55] of the island of Vasiladi in the lagune of Mesolonghi, and wished to reduce the fortress of Anatolico. In spite of his better judgment, Church deferred to his colleague's desire, postponed his own design, and assisted in an expedition against Anatolico, which, owing to a fatal miscalculation of the defences,[56] was unsuccessful. Upon this, Hastings hurriedly retreated to Dragomestre, whither, after providing for the defence of Vasiladi, Church followed. The failure was embittered by a misunderstanding between the two commanders, which, though afterwards corrected, deprived the army of Hastings's co-operation for a while.[57] Whatever differences

[53] *E.g.* in January 1,000 Rumeliots were promised, but never came; in May 1,200 Peloponnesians, never came; in June 2,000 men with artillery, never came; in July 3,000 men countermanded, to lie idle at Megara, and only 250 arrived in the following April, &c. As to money, all the president sent was 14,000 francs, 20,000 dollars, and 150,000 piastres—say 7,000*l.*—with which to keep and pay 3,000 officers and men for more than a year. In January 1828 the pay of the men had been in arrears since March 1827. In November 1828, again, they had been four months without pay.

[54] Sir R. Church to Captain Hastings, 12 Dec. 1827. Reports to President, 18 and 22 February.

[55] Captain Hastings to Sir R. Church, 21 Dec. 1827.

[56] Captain Hastings to Sir R. Church, 4 Jan. 1828.

[57] 'Captain Hastings, who possessed the noblest qualities of the head and heart, had unfortunately a hastiness of temper and manner which at times rendered co-operation with him difficult. At Vasiladi a misunderstanding took place between him

may have subsisted between them, the general and Hastings loyally co-operated in the second fruitless attack upon Anatolico, made at the president's urgent solicitation, when the gallant seaman received the mortal wound (25 May) which broke up the siege.

During the summer of 1828 little was done by the small army in western Greece, which had indeed enough to do to keep itself alive at all, so dire was its distress for lack of food, clothes, and shelter. It was now stationed at the entrenched camp of Mitika, as being more convenient than Dragomestre for the movements now in contemplation against Prevesa and the gulf of Arta. The roadstead was good, and the neighbourhood of the Ionian island of Kalamo, where many Greek families had taken refuge, was an advantage. Church established various positions in the mountains and harassed the communications of the enemy. The Turks held their line of fortified posts from Arta to Mesolonghi, and, though more than once threatening to advance, never ventured upon a serious attack, in which they could hardly have failed of success. The Greek army was suffered, as Church wrote, to 'take root;' and rooted it remained on the coast until reinforcements and a flotilla should render more active measures practicable. President Capodistrias visited the camp in person in July, reviewed the troops with apparent satisfaction, approved (15 July) the general's plan of occupying the gulf of Arta and the Makrinoros, and promised the

---

and the general-in-chief which led to a disagreeable correspondence between them and probably to the want of success of the operation attempted against Anatolico on this occasion. The misunderstanding arose in the first instance on the general expressing surprise at being invited by Captain Hastings to pay him 2,000 dollars after the reduction of Vasiladi, as a remuneration to the crews of the vessels employed against that place; in the next place, on a question of sending boats for some troops. The commander of the naval forces conceived that the general was interfering with his department, and expressed himself to that effect in a way which produced a quick reply. Both officers having the good of the service at heart, this unpleasant affair was soon terminated amicably. It must be said to the honour of Captain Hastings that he had put himself to great inconvenience for a considerable time past in providing resources from his own funds for paying the crew of the steam-vessel under his orders, and he was at this moment so far disgusted with the little attention paid to his wants by the provisional government, that it had affected his mind considerably; and to this feeling must be attributed his intemperate conduct at Vasiladi.' There were no funds wherewith to meet Hastings's demand for 2,000 dollars. This is Church's own account of the quarrel. It is clear, however, from Hastings's letter (printed in Finlay, *History of Greece*, vii. 344-5) that other disputes occurred, arising from the dishonesty of some of the Greek chiefs, who appear to have sold their rations at a time when every ounce of flour was precious. That Church countenanced such proceedings is of course impossible to believe, but it is far from unlikely that his trustful nature was imposed upon by the proverbial duplicity of the Greeks.

F 2

reinforcements necessary to raise the army to 6,000 men.'⁵⁸ Yet it was not until 16 September that the long-expected flotilla arrived, and even then 'not a soldier or a gun was sent to the land force, though more than 8,000 men were being drilled and paraded in the camp at Megara.'

Church resolved to wait no longer for reinforcements that would apparently never come, and in defiance of the president's order to postpone all military operations pending the conferences of the allies then being held at Poros, he opened the campaign with his 2,000 half-starved soldiers and four field-pieces, early in October. Moving upon the gulf of Arta in two divisions (the second commanded by Baron Dentzel), and valiantly supported by the flotilla of two steamers, a gunboat, and some Hydriot mistikos, which forced the entrance to the gulf, under the fire of the batteries of Prevesa and Punta, and defeated or captured the Turkish gunboats, Church seized and garrisoned Koronisi, beat back two assaults of the Turks of Arta, and made himself master of the gulf. Dentzel and Zavellas then struck inland, drove the Turks out of the provinces of Apokoros and Kravari, and seized the mountain road which crosses the Pindus to Trikkala ; but were recalled by the president, whose orders were peremptory that no further advance should be made beyond the line of the Makrinoros. Meanwhile Church laid siege to Vonitza, an important post commanding the way from Prevesa to Akarnania :

> On Christmas Day an order of the day was given out fixing the assault for the next day, and forbidding plunder of the town or ill-treatment of defenceless inhabitants, and an unanimous promise was made by the soldiery to that effect. On the 27th the assault was made by the soldiers in three divisions, and by the seamen from the boats : the fighting was hot ; but the town was taken, and the Albanian garrison was driven out and shut up in the castle. After the capture, the troops faithfully kept

---

⁵⁸ It is not necessary here to review the conduct and policy of Capodistrias ; but, while there can be no doubt that he neglected to support Church and repeatedly broke his promises of supplies and reinforcement it is only fair to add that the president was in n extremely difficult position, and his conduct was often guided by the hard dictates of necessity. Especially awkward was it for him to have to discuss measures for the pacification of Greece with the ambassadors of the three allies at Poros, when an armistice was supposed to exist and the French army was peaceably expelling the Egyptians from the Peloponnesus, and at the same time to have to support, or appear to support, the generalissimo of the Greek army, who was bent upon active hostilities, despite all armistices and all diplomatic negotiations. There is no doubt, moreover, that his visit to Church's camp in July had impressed him with a strong feeling against the wild disorganised bands of *palikari* who passed there as soldiers.

their promise, the evacuation of the town was carried out under the protection of the soldiers and sailors, and the garrison of the castle abstained from firing until the evacuation was complete. But the castle of Vonitza still held out in hopes of the promised relief from Prevesa. Lines were drawn across the promontory of Actium, and manned and armed by the Greek soldiers to meet the threatened attack of the Seraskier. He made two attempts in February, by sea and land, but was driven back upon Punta, and finally repulsed he retired to Prevesa. The castle capitulated on honourable terms, on 17 March, 1829, and the Albanian garrison of 300 men was conducted safely to Punta.

As soon as this important post was gained, the general directed all his efforts to an immediate advance upon the Makrinoros. The Makrinoros is the range of mountains and forest wedged in between the head of the gulf of Arta and the deep-sunk bed of the Aspropotamos on the east, falling down on the north-west side to Kombotti and the plain of Arta, and running up north to join Mount Djumerka and the Epirote chain; overlooking on the south the lakes of Ambrakia, and Ozeros, and the Aspropotamos. The castle of Kervasara, lying at the foot of the mountain, and in the south-eastern angle of the gulf, is the gate to the mountain passes from Akarnania and the south. A road at the foot of the cliffs, rough and precipitous, 'forms a pass like that of the Syrian Gates, at the head of the bay of Scanderoon,' and winds along for a day's journey by Menidhi to Kombotti on the plain of Arta; other roads cross the mountain to Arta, and to Agrafa, and the Aspropotamos. Information had reached the general that a convoy was at Kombotti, waiting for an escort to cross the mountain to Kervasara. Leaving a garrison in Vonitza, and some men to threaten Kervasara, he embarked by night, 25 March, with a detachment from Lutraki in the boats of the flotilla, landed at Menidhi, midway on the cliff road, and seized the stations on the road, while the boats went back to fetch another detachment. The men climbing the western ravines during the night, surprised at daybreak a Turkish outpost on the heights and drove them into the fortified post on the plateau, the Paleo Castro of Makrinoros. Another body had been ordered to make a circuit round Kervasara, and to advance as skirmishers up the southern face of the mountain; these finding the lower posts unoccupied, pressed onwards to the ridge and closed round the Paleo Castro on the south side. Through the course of the night and next morning the boats brought over fresh men from Lutraki, and with these the general occupied the heads of the ravines leading down to the plain of Arta, and sent forward a division to occupy the plateau of Langadha, which commands the eastern slopes to the valley of the Aspropotamos. . . . The Turks had been completely surprised by the rapidity of the movement. That very day a convoy of provisions and money for Kervasara and Mesolonghi was to have crossed the mountains, and troops from Kervasara had come up to the fortified post on the ridge to meet the escort on its way, and to conduct it. But the roads on both sides of the mountain had been seized by the Greeks, and the Turks found their way barred, without having means of knowing what was the strength of the enemy which was on their road. The Greeks, increasing in numbers as the boats brought up fresh men from Lutraki, blockaded the garrison in the tower; guns were brought up, the tower bombarded by heavy guns from the gunboats, and on 29 March the garrison surrendered on promise of safe-conduct.

The way over the mountain being secured, and all supplies cut off from the garrisons on the south side, their surrender was merely a question of time. The Turks at Prevesa made no effort to save them, and Kervasara, the gate of the province of Valtos, capitulated on 7 April. The general then pushed forward along the ridges between Kervasara and the fords of the Aspropotamos, and a division was ordered to prepare to march on Mesolonghi, while he himself returned to protect his position on the Makrinoros from a probable attack of the Turks in Arta. As the result of these measures Lepanto surrendered on 30 April, 1829, and Mesolonghi and Anatolico on 17 May; when

the last body of Turkish troops was escorted by Varnakiotti and a division of General Church's army through Akarnania to the gulf of Arta and Prevesa, on their return to Albania. The evacuation of Akarnania and Aetolia was now complete; and the Greeks held actual possession by the force of their own arms of the natural frontiers of the western provinces—the gulf of Arta and the Makrinoros defiles.

In June Sir Richard Church entered Mesolonghi as the true liberator of western Greece.

His work was done. He had marked out for himself, two years before, a plan of operations. He had tenaciously adhered to his purpose, and successfully carried it out amidst discouragement, and opposition, and countless difficulties. For eighteen months he had been at the head of his bands of Rumeliot *palikari*, sharing their rough camp life, never complaining, except for the wants of his men; making the best of them, keeping them together, and leading them to success; settling their quarrels, and restraining their lawlessness by the justice and integrity and chivalrous bearing of an English officer. It was no slight mark of the influence he had acquired over his men that, after their savage warfare of years with the Turks, he was able to make them humane and generous in their treatment of enemies. Bounties were given for Turkish prisoners instead of Turkish heads; cattle taken from Greeks on the Turkish side were restored or paid for; respect towards the enemy was enforced in all communications and interviews that passed between the camps; the most generous treatment of the Albanian officers and men was shown after capitulation, and in each case the garrisons were conducted in safety through the Greek camp without molestation or insult.[59]

His final triumph was somewhat marred by the petty jealousy of the president, who seized the moment of Church's success to appoint his own brother Agostino Capodistrias—who can only be described as a contemptible fool—lieutenant plenipotentiary in western Greece. Agostino was at the time ornamentally parading at Lepanto a large force of troops which was sorely needed to guard the frontier; and so it happened that the man who received the capitulation of Mesolonghi was not that 'liege lord of Philhellenes' (to use Finlay's phrase) who had toiled and conquered, but the puny nonentity who happened to be the brother of John Capodistrias. The general protested against the insult, but no slight would have induced him to abandon his duty. His work, however, was accomplished; western Greece was practically freed from the Turkish domination, though he had to wait some time before he saw the fruits of his successful struggle. With a clear conscience he attended the National Assembly at Argos, 25 August 1829, and there resigned the command which had been conferred upon him two years before, 'with an indignant protest against the way in which the government of Capodistrias had neglected the army and thwarted military operations.'

If it be asked, what was the result of Church's liberation of western Greece? the answer may be given in the words of one who, in his 'History of Greece,' has striven his utmost to discredit Sir Richard's services. Finlay was not always so grudging of appreciation, and about 1840 he wrote to the general:

I well recollect the landing at Dragomestre, which at the time I thought a desperate and even hopeless attempt with the small force you had. I have long, however, seen that it was to that desperate step that Greece owes the extension of her frontier. The 500 men induced Romeli to take arms, and prevented Capodistrias making the Morea Greece. You gave him Romeli in spite of himself, and you made Agostino a hero.

In other words, had western Greece not been Greek when the frontier was being mapped out by the allies, the kingdom of Greece would have been limited (as Lord Aberdeen and Capodistrias desired) to the Peloponnesus. The protocol of 3 Feb. 1830, 'in deference to the desire expressed by the Porte,' had surrendered these very provinces which he had conquered, and by

[59] C. M. Church, l.c. 13-16.

the frontier line then drawn had excluded from free Greece the men of Akarnania and Aetolia. This called forth from Church, in April 1830, an indignant letter, which was published in England with a preface by Wilmot Horton, who described it as 'the simple protest of a soldier who, in this breathing time of nations, has pursued an unnoticed but not less brilliant career with a firmness and self-devotion worthy of the brightest periods of European history.'[60] He could not keep silence. His recollections were too fresh, as he said, of the efforts which had been made by the men under his command to emancipate these provinces from the Turkish yoke. They had given back to Greece her glorious Mesolonghi. He had witnessed their joy at liberation—the happy meeting of women and children restored to their fathers, husbands, brothers, and to their homes, after nine years of desolation. He had heard their solemn and hearty thanks offered up to the Almighty, and seen the fierce Albanians, on leaving the country in which they had been fairly overcome, partaking of the bread of their conquerors, embracing them gratefully for the good treatment they had received at their hands, and declaring that the Greeks had a right to enjoy the country they had won. So he recorded his solemn protest :

It is impossible [he wrote] to describe the despair of the people of this country on the intimation that the limits of Greece, according to the new protocol, would exclude the whole of Akarnania and a part of Aetolia. . . . I cannot believe that the generous interference of the allied powers is to be brought to a conclusion by entailing upon Greece disasters of the most serious nature—that, instead of giving her a frontier, they are about to take one from her. . . . Lulled into a fatal security by the protocol of 22 March, the Greeks were unanimous in their gratitude to the allied powers, and saw before them a fair prospect of becoming an independent country, in the supposition that their frontier would be that of the line from Volo to Arta. . . . This line and, far beyond it, the cantons of Agrafa and the province of Aspropotamos are in the peaceable possession of the Greeks ; and, before I left the camp of Makrinoros, we had fortified its passes on the highroads leading from Trikkala, Arta, Prevesa, and Joannina, to Vonitza, Mesolonghi, Lepanto, Salona, &c.

Are these people to be again given up to the Turks after having fought for their liberty for nine years, and being ever the foremost in every glorious exertion for the general emancipation of their country and of Greece in general? Will they submit to the Turks as their masters? From the knowledge that I have of their characters, and from what they have suffered, I think they never will. Can the other Greeks, or ought

---

[60] *Observations on an Eligible Line of Frontier for Greece.* Ridgway, 1830.

the other Greeks, to abandon them to their miserable fate? I doubt it; and what may not be apprehended from the desperate resolution of some thousands of determined and veteran soldiers? Blood will doubtless flow before these men give up their country, their families, and their honour into the hands of the Turks.

The frontier for which he pleaded was granted to Greece two years afterwards. The frontier imposed in 1830 was rectified in 1832 by the efforts of Lord Palmerston and Sir Stratford Canning; the boundaries from the gulf of Volo to the gulf of Arta were then laid down, and the provinces which Church had won for the Greeks were finally restored to them.

Here the military career of Sir Richard Church comes to a worthy end. For forty years more he lived at Athens, beloved and respected by all who reverenced a loyal and upright character; and there he died in 1873, in his ninetieth year, the centre of a wide circle of friends, who delighted in being honoured with the confidence of 'the liege lord of Philhellenes.' The recollections of his self-sacrificing and chivalrous career, stories of his justice, integrity, and kindness, his hardihood and endurance, long lingered among his Greek soldiers and contemporaries. To later generations the epitaph on his monument raised by the Greek nation in the cemetery at Athens will be his abiding memorial:

RICHARD CHURCH,

GENERAL,

WHO, HAVING GIVEN HIMSELF AND ALL THAT HE HAD

TO RESCUE A CHRISTIAN RACE

FROM OPPRESSION,

AND TO MAKE GREECE A NATION,

LIVED FOR HER SERVICE,

AND DIED AMONGST HER PEOPLE,

RESTS HERE IN PEACE AND FAITH.

1873.

BY THE SAME AUTHOR.

THE LIFE OF STRATFORD CANNING,
VISCOUNT STRATFORD DE REDCLIFFE, K.G.
From his Private and Official Papers. With Three
Portraits. Two volumes. 36s.

POPULAR EDITION (Abridged). 1 vol. 7s. 6d.

London: LONGMANS, GREEN, & CO.

PRINTED BY
SPOTTISWOODE AND CO., NEW-STREET SQUARE
LONDON

39 Paternoster Row, London, E.C.
November 1890.

A Catalogue of Works
IN
GENERAL LITERATURE
PUBLISHED BY
MESSRS. LONGMANS, GREEN, & CO.

MESSRS. LONGMANS, GREEN, & CO.

Issue the undermentioned Lists of their Publications, which may be had post free on application:—

1. Monthly List of New Works and New Editions.
2. Quarterly List of Announcements and New Works.
3. Notes on Books; being an Analysis of the Works published during each Quarter.
4. Catalogue of Scientific Works.
5. Catalogue of Medical and Surgical Works.
6. Catalogue of School Books and Educational Works.
7. Catalogue of Books for Elementary Schools and Pupil Teachers.
8. Catalogue of Theological Works by Divines and Members of the Church of England.
9. Catalogue of Works in General Literature.

ABBEY and OVERTON.—The English Church in the Eighteenth Century. By CHARLES J. ABBEY and JOHN H. OVERTON. Cr. 8vo. 7s. 6d.

ABBOTT.—Hellenica. A Collection of Essays on Greek Poetry, Philosophy, History, and Religion. Edited by EVELYN ABBOTT, M.A. LL.D. Fellow and Tutor of Balliol College, Oxford. 8vo. 16s.

ABBOTT (Evelyn, M.A. LL.D.) — Works by.

A Skeleton Outline of Greek History. Chronologically Arranged. Crown 8vo. 2s. 6d.

A History of Greece. In Two Parts.
Part I.—From the Earliest Times to the Ionian Revolt. Crown 8vo. 10s. 6d.
Part II. Vol. I.—500-445 B.C. [*In the press.*]
Vol. II.—[*In preparation.*]

ACLAND and RANSOME.—A Handbook in Outline of the Political History of England to 1887. Chronologically Arranged. By A. H. DYKE ACLAND, M.P. and CYRIL RANSOME, M.A. Crown 8vo. 6s.

ACTON.—Modern Cookery. By ELIZA ACTON. With 150 Woodcuts. Fcp. 8vo. 4s. 6d.

A. K. H. B.—The Essays and Contributions of. Cr. 8vo.

Autumn Holidays of a Country Parson. 3s. 6d.
Changed Aspects of Unchanged Truths. 3s. 6d.
Commonplace Philosopher. 3s. 6d.
Counsel and Comfort from a City Pulpit. 3s. 6d.
Critical Essays of a Country Parson. 3s. 6d.
East Coast Days and Memories. 3s. 6d.

[*Continued on next page.*

A

A. K. H. B.—The Essays and Contributions of—*continued*.
  Graver Thoughts of a Country Parson. Three Series. 3s. 6d. each.
  Landscapes, Churches, and Moralities. 3s. 6d.
  Leisure Hours in Town. 3s. 6d.
  Lessons of Middle Age. 3s. 6d.
  Our Little Life. Two Series. 3s. 6d. each.
  Our Homely Comedy and Tragedy. 3s. 6d.
  Present Day Thoughts. 3s. 6d.
  Recreations of a Country Parson. Three Series. 3s. 6d. each.
  Seaside Musings. 3s. 6d.
  Sunday Afternoons in the Parish Church of a Scottish University City. 3s. 6d.
  'To Meet the Day' through the Christian Year: being a Text of Scripture, with an Original Meditation and a Short Selection in Verse for Every Day. 4s. 6d.

American Whist, Illustrated: containing the Laws and Principles of the Game, the Analysis of the New Play and American Leads, and a Series of Hands in Diagram, and combining Whist Universal and American Whist. By G. W. P. Fcp. 8vo. 6s. 6d.

AMOS.—A Primer of the English Constitution and Government. By SHELDON AMOS. Crown 8vo. 6s.

Annual Register (The). A Review of Public Events at Home and Abroad, for the year 1889. 8vo. 18s.
  * Volumes of the 'Annual Register' for the years 1863-1888 can still be had.

ANSTEY.—Works by F. Anstey, Author of 'Vice Versâ.'
  The Black Poodle, and other Stories. Crown 8vo. 2s. bds.; 2s. 6d. cl.
  Voces Populi. Reprinted from *Punch.* With 20 Illustrations by J. BERNARD PARTRIDGE. Fcp. 4to. 5s.

ARISTOTLE.—The Works of.
  The Politics, G. Bekker's Greek Text of Books I. III. IV. (VII.) with an English Translation by W. E. BOLLAND, M.A.; and short Introductory Essays by A. LANG, M.A. Cr. 8vo. 7s. 6d.
  The Politics: Introductory Essays. By ANDREW LANG. (From Bolland and Lang's 'Politics.') Crown 8vo. 2s. 6d.
  The Ethics; Greek Text, illustrated with Essays and Notes. By Sir ALEXANDER GRANT, Bart. M.A. LL.D. 2 vols. 8vo. 32s.
  The Nicomachean Ethics, Newly Translated into English. By ROBERT WILLIAMS, Barrister-at-Law. Crown 8vo. 7s. 6d.

ARMSTRONG (G. F.)—Works by.
  Poems: Lyrical and Dramatic. Fcp. 8vo. 6s.
  King Saul. (The Tragedy of Israel, Part I.) Fcp. 8vo. 5s.
  King David. (The Tragedy of Israel, Part II.) Fcp. 8vo. 6s.
  King Solomon. (The Tragedy of Israel, Part III.) Fcp. 8vo. 6s.
  Ugone: A Tragedy. Fcp. 8vo. 6s.
  A Garland from Greece; Poems. Fcp. 8vo. 9s.
  Stories of Wicklow; Poems. Fcp. 8vo. 9s.
  Victoria Regina et Imperatrix: a Jubilee Song from Ireland, 1887. 4to. 2s. 6d.
  Mephistopheles in Broadcloth: a Satire. Fcp. 8vo. 4s.
  The Life and Letters of Edmund J. Armstrong. Fcp. 8vo. 7s. 6d.

ARMSTRONG (E. J.)—Works by.
  Poetical Works. Fcp. 8vo. 5s.
  Essays and Sketches. Fcp. 8vo. 5s.

ARNOLD. — The Light of the World: a Poem. By Sir EDWIN ARNOLD, K.C.I.E. Crown 8vo. 7s. 6d. net.

ARNOLD (Dr. T.)—Works by.
  Introductory Lectures on Modern History. 8vo. 7s. 6d.
  Sermons Preached mostly in the Chapel of Rugby School. 6 vols. crown 8vo. 30s. or separately, 5s. ea.
  Miscellaneous Works. 8vo. 7s. 6d.

ASHLEY.—English Economic History and Theory. By W. J. ASHLEY, M.A. Professor of Political Economy in the University of Toronto.
  Part I.—The Middle Ages. 5s.

Atelier (The) du Lys; or, an Art Student in the Reign of Terror. By the Author of 'Mademoiselle Mori.' Crown 8vo. 2s. 6d.

    BY THE SAME AUTHOR.
Mademoiselle Mori: a Tale of Modern Rome. Crown 8vo. 2s. 6d.
That Child. Illustrated by GORDON BROWNE. Crown 8vo. 3s. 6d.

Atelier (The) du Lys Works by the Author of—*continued*.

Under a Cloud. Crown 8vo. 5s.

The Fiddler of Lugau. With Illustrations by W. RALSTON. Crown 8vo. 6s.

A Child of the Revolution. With Illustrations by C. J. STANILAND. Crown 8vo. 6s.

Hester's Venture: a Novel. Crown 8vo. 2s. 6d.

In the Olden Time: a Tale of the Peasant War in Germany. Crown. 8vo. 2s. 6d.

BACON.—The Works and Life of.

Complete Works. Edited by R. L. ELLIS, J. SPEDDING, and D. D. HEATH. 7 vols. 8vo. £3. 13s. 6d.

Letters and Life, including all his Occasional Works. Edited by J. SPEDDING. 7 vols. 8vo. £4. 4s.

The Essays; with Annotations. By RICHARD WHATELY, D.D., 8vo. 10s. 6d.

The Essays; with **Introduction,** Notes, and Index. By E. A. ABBOTT, D.D. 2 vols. fcp. 8vo. price 6s. Text and Index only, without **Introduction** and Notes, in 1 vol. fcp. 8vo. 2s. 6d.

The BADMINTON LIBRARY, edited by the DUKE OF BEAUFORT, K.G., assisted by ALFRED E. T. WATSON.

Hunting. By the DUKE OF BEAUFORT, K.G. and MOWBRAY MORRIS. With 53 Illus. by J. Sturgess, J. Charlton, and A. M. Biddulph. Crown 8vo. 10s. 6d.

Fishing. By H. CHOLMONDELEY-PENNELL.
Vol. I. Salmon, **Trout,** and Grayling. With 158 Illustrations. Cr. 8vo. 10s. 6d.
Vol. II. Pike and other Coarse **Fish.** With 132 Illustrations. Cr. 8vo. 10s. 6d.

Racing and Steeplechasing. By the EARL OF SUFFOLK AND BERKSHIRE, W. G. CRAVEN, &c. With 56 Illustrations by J. Sturgess. Cr. 8vo. 10s. 6d.

Shooting. By Lord WALSINGHAM and Sir RALPH PAYNE-GALLWEY, Bart.
Vol. I. Field and Covert. With 105 Illustrations. Cr. 8vo. 10s. 6d.
Vol. II. Moor and Marsh. With 65 Illustrations. Cr. 8vo. 10s. 6d.

The BADMINTON LIBRARY—*continued*.

Cycling. By VISCOUNT BURY, K.C.M.G. and G. LACY HILLIER. With 19 Plates and 61 Woodcuts by Viscount Bury and Joseph Pennell. Cr. 8vo. 10s. 6d.

Athletics and Football. By MONTAGUE SHEARMAN. With 6 full-page Illustrations and 45 Woodcuts by Stanley Berkeley, and from Photographs by G. Mitchell. Cr. 8vo. 10s. 6d.

Boating. By W. B. WOODGATE. With 10 full-page Illustrations and 39 Woodcuts in the Text. Cr. 8vo. 10s. 6d.

Cricket. By A. G. STEEL and the Hon. R. H. LYTTELTON. With 11 full-page Illustrations and 52 Woodcuts in the Text, by Lucien Davis. Cr. 8vo. 10s. 6d.

Driving. By the DUKE OF BEAUFORT. With 11 Plates and 54 Woodcuts by J. Sturgess and G. D. Giles. Cr. 8vo. 10s. 6d.

Fencing, Boxing, and Wrestling. By WALTER H. POLLOCK, F. C. GROVE, C. PREVOST, E. B. MICHELL, and WALTER ARMSTRONG. With 18 Plates and 24 Woodcuts. Crown 8vo. 10s. 6d.

Golf. By HORACE HUTCHINSON, the Rt. Hon. A. J. BALFOUR, M.P. ANDREW LANG, Sir W. G. SIMPSON, Bart. &c. With 19 Plates and 69 Woodcuts. Crown 8vo. 10s. 6d.

Tennis, Lawn Tennis, Rackets, and Fives. By J. M. and C. G. HEATHCOTE, E. O. PLEYDELL-BOUVERIE, and A. C. AINGER. With 12 Plates and 67 Woodcuts, &c. Crown 8vo. 10s. 6d.

BAGEHOT (Walter)—Works by.

Biographical Studies. 8vo. 12s.

Economic Studies. 8vo. 10s. 6d.

Literary Studies. 2 vols. 8vo. 28s.

The Postulates of English Political Economy. Cr. 8vo. 2s. 6d.

A Practical Plan for Assimilating the English and American Money as a Step towards a Universal Money. Cr. 8vo. 2s. 6d.

BAGWELL.— Ireland under the Tudors, with a Succinct Account of the Earlier History. By RICHARD BAGWELL, M.A. (3 vols.) Vols. I. and II. From the first invasion of the Northmen to the year 1578. 8vo. 32s. Vol. III. 1578-1603. 8vo. 18s.

BAIN (Alexander)—Works by.
  Mental and Moral Science. Crown 8vo. 10s. 6d.
  Senses and the Intellect. 8vo. 15s.
  Emotions and the Will. 8vo. 15s.
  Logic, Deductive and Inductive. PART I. *Deduction*, 4s. PART II. *Induction*, 6s. 6d.
  Practical Essays. Cr. 8vo. 2s.

BAKER.—By the Western Sea: a Summer Idyll. By JAMES BAKER, F.R.G.S. Author of 'John Westacott.' Cr. 8vo. 6s.

BAKER. — 'War with Crime': being a Selection of Reprinted Papers on Crime, Prison Discipline, &c. By T. BARWICK LL. BAKER. 8vo. 12s. 6d.

BAKER (Sir S. W.)—Works by.
  Eight Years in Ceylon. With 6 Illustrations. Crown 8vo. 3s. 6d.
  The Rifle and the Hound in Ceylon. With 6 Illustrations. Crown 8vo. 3s. 6d.

BALL (The Rt. Hon. J. T.)—Works by.
  The Reformed Church of Ireland (1537-1886). 8vo. 7s. 6d.
  Historical Review of the Legislative Systems Operative in Ireland, from the Invasion of Henry the Second to the Union (1172-1800). 8vo. 6s.

BEACONSFIELD (The Earl of)— Works by.
  Novels and Tales. The Hughenden Edition. With 2 Portraits and 11 Vignettes. 11 vols. Crown 8vo. 42s.

Endymion.	Henrietta Temple.
Lothair.	Contarini Fleming, &c.
Coningsby.	Alroy, Ixion, &c.
Tancred. Sybil.	The Young Duke, &c.
Venetia.	Vivian Grey.

  Novels and Tales. Cheap Edition. complete in 11 vols. Crown 8vo. 1s. each, boards; 1s. 6d. each, cloth.

BECKER (Professor)—Works by.
  Gallus; or, Roman Scenes in the Time of Augustus. Post 8vo. 7s. 6d.
  Charicles; or, Illustrations of the Private Life of the Ancient Greeks. Post 8vo. 7s. 6d.

BELL.—Will o' the Wisp: a Story. By Mrs. HUGH BELL. Illustrated by E. L. SHUTE. Crown 8vo. 3s. 6d.

BLAKE.—Tables for the Conversion of 5 per Cent. Interest from $\frac{1}{16}$ to 7 per Cent. By J. BLAKE, of the London Joint Stock Bank, Limited. 8vo. 12s. 6d.

Book (The) of Wedding Days. Arranged on the Plan of a Birthday Book. With 96 Illustrated Borders, Frontispiece, and Title-page by WALTER CRANE; and Quotations for each Day Compiled and Arranged by K. E. J. REID, MAY ROSS, and MABEL BAMFIELD. 4to. 21s.

BOWEN.—Thirty Years of Colonial Government: a Selection from the Official Papers of the Rt. Hon. Sir George Ferguson Bowen, G.C.M.G. D.C.L. LL.D. &c. Edited by STANLEY LANE-POOLE. 2 vols. 8vo. 32s.

BRASSEY (Lady)—Works by.
  A Voyage in the 'Sunbeam,' our Home on the Ocean for Eleven Months.
    Library Edition. With 8 Maps and Charts, and 118 Illustrations, 8vo. 21s.
    Cabinet Edition. With Map and 66 Illustrations, crown 8vo. 7s. 6d.
    School Edition. With 37 Illustrations, fcp. 2s. cloth, or 3s. white parchment.
    Popular Edition. With 60 Illustrations, 4to. 6d. sewed, 1s. cloth.

  Sunshine and Storm in the East.
    Library Edition. With 2 Maps and 114 Illustrations, 8vo. 21s.
    Cabinet Edition. With 2 Maps and 114 Illustrations, crown 8vo. 7s. 6d.
    Popular Edition. With 103 Illustrations, 4to. 6d. sewed, 1s. cloth.

  In the Trades, the Tropics, and the 'Roaring Forties.'
    Cabinet Edition. With Map and 220 Illustrations, crown 8vo. 7s. 6d.
    Popular Edition. With 183 Illustrations, 4to. 6d. sewed, 1s. cloth.

BRASSEY (Lady) — Works by — *continued*.

The Last Voyage to India and Australia in the 'Sunbeam.' With Charts and Maps, and 40 Illustrations in Monotone (20 full-page), and nearly 200 Illustrations in the Text from Drawings by R. T. PRITCHETT. 8vo. 21*s*.

Three Voyages in the 'Sunbeam.' Popular Edition. With 346 Illustrations, 4to. 2*s*. 6*d*.

BRAY.—The Philosophy of Necessity ; or, Law in Mind as in Matter. By CHARLES BRAY. Crown 8vo. 5*s*.

BRIGHT.—A History of England. By the Rev. J. FRANCK BRIGHT, D.D. Master of University College, Oxford. 4 vols. crown 8vo.
Period I.—Mediæval Monarchy : The Departure of the Romans to Richard III. From A.D. 449 to 1485. 4*s*. 6*d*.
Period II.—Personal Monarchy : Henry VII. to James II. From 1485 to 1688. 5*s*.
Period III.—Constitutional Monarchy : William and Mary to William IV. From 1689 to 1837. 7*s*. 6*d*.
Period IV.—The Growth of Democracy : Victoria. From 1837 to 1880. 6*s*.

BRYDEN. — Kloof and Karroo : Sport, Legend, and Natural History in Cape Colony. By H. A. BRYDEN. With 17 Illustrations. 8vo. 10*s*. 6*d*.

BUCKLE. — History of Civilisation in England and France, Spain and Scotland. By HENRY THOMAS BUCKLE. 3 vols. cr. 8vo. 24*s*.

BUCKTON (Mrs. C. M.)—Works by.
Food and Home Cookery. With 11 Woodcuts. Crown 8vo. 2*s*. 6*d*.
Health in the House. With 41 Woodcuts and Diagrams. Crown 8vo. 2*s*.

BULL (Thomas)—Works by.
Hints to Mothers on the Management of their Health during the Period of Pregnancy. Fcp. 8vo. 1*s*. 6*d*.
The Maternal Management of Children in Health and Disease. Fcp. 8vo. 1*s*. 6*d*.

BUTLER (Samuel)—Works by.
Op. 1. Erewhon. Cr. 8vo. 5*s*.
Op. 2. The Fair Haven. A Work in Defence of the Miraculous Element in our Lord's Ministry. Cr. 8vo. 7*s*. 6*d*.
Op. 3. Life and Habit. An Essay after a Completer View of Evolution. Cr. 8vo. 7*s*. 6*d*.
Op. 4. Evolution, Old and New. Cr. 8vo. 10*s*. 6*d*.
Op. 5. Unconscious Memory. Cr. 8vo. 7*s*. 6*d*.
Op. 6. Alps and Sanctuaries of Piedmont and the Canton Ticino. Illustrated. Pott 4to. 10*s*. 6*d*.
Op. 7. Selections from Ops. 1–6. With Remarks on Mr. G. J. ROMANES' 'Mental Evolution in Animals.' Cr. 8vo. 7*s*. 6*d*.
Op. 8. Luck, or Cunning, as the Main Means of Organic Modification ? Cr. 8vo. 7*s*. 6*d*.
Op. 9. Ex Voto. An Account of the Sacro Monte or New Jerusalem at Varallo-Sesia. 10*s*. 6*d*.
Holbein's 'La Danse.' A Note on a Drawing called 'La Danse.' 3*s*.

CARLYLE. — Thomas Carlyle : a History of his Life. By J. A. FROUDE. 1795-1835, 2 vols. crown 8vo. 7*s*. 1834-1881, 2 vols. crown 8vo. 7*s*.

CASE. — Physical Realism : being an Analytical Philosophy from the Physical Objects of Science to the Physical Data of Sense. By THOMAS CASE, M.A. Fellow and Senior Tutor C.C.C. 8vo. 15*s*.

CHETWYND. — Racing Reminiscences and Experiences of the Turf. By Sir GEORGE CHETWYND, Bart. 8vo.

CHILD. — Church and State under the Tudors. By GILBERT W. CHILD, M.A. Exeter College, Oxford. 8vo. 15*s*.

CHISHOLM.—Handbook of Commercial Geography. By G. G. CHISHOLM, B.Sc. With 29 Maps. 8vo. 16*s*.

CHURCH.—Sir Richard Church, C.B. G.C.H. Commander-in-Chief of the Greeks in the War of Independence: a Memoir. By STANLEY LANE-POOLE, Author of 'The Life of Viscount Stratford de Redcliffe.' With 2 Plans. 8vo. 5s.

CLARK-KENNEDY.—Pictures in Rhyme. By ARTHUR CLARK-KENNEDY. With Illustrations by MAURICE GREIFFENHAGEN. Cr. 8vo.

Clavers, the Despot's Champion: a Scots Biography. By A SOUTHERN. Crown 8vo. 7s. 6d.

CLODD.—The Story of Creation: a Plain Account of Evolution. By EDWARD CLODD. With 77 Illustrations. Crown 8vo. 3s. 6d.

CLUTTERBUCK.—The Skipper in Arctic Seas. By W. J CLUTTERBUCK, one of the Authors of 'Three in Norway.' With 39 Illustrations. Cr. 8vo. 10s. 6d.

COLENSO.—The Pentateuch and Book of Joshua Critically Examined. By J. W. COLENSO, D.D. late Bishop of Natal. Crown 8vo. 6s.

COLMORE.—A Living Epitaph. By G. COLMORE, Author of 'A Conspiracy of Silence' &c. Crown 8vo. 6s.

Comic (The) Birthday Book. Edited by W. F MARCH-PHILLIPPS. 32mo. 1s. 6d. cloth gilt.

COMYN.—Atherstone Priory: a Tale. By L. N. COMYN. Cr. 8vo. 2s. 6d.

CONINGTON (John)—Works by.

The Æneid of Virgil. Translated into English Verse. Crown 8vo. 6s.

The Poems of Virgil. Translated into English Prose. Crown 8vo. 6s.

COOLIDGE.—Swiss Travel and Swiss Guide-Books. By W. A. B. COOLIDGE, Fellow of Magdalen College, Oxford. Crown 8vo. 10s. 6d.

COURTHOPE.—The Paradise of Birds. By WILLIAM JOHN COURTHOPE. With Illustrations by LANCELOT SPEED. Royal 8vo. 7s. 6d.

COX.—A General History of Greece, from the Earliest Period to the Death of Alexander the Great; with a sketch of the subsequent History to the Present Time. By the Rev. Sir G. W. COX, Bart. M.A. With 11 Maps and Plans. Crown 8vo. 7s. 6d.

CRAKE.—Historical Tales. By A. D. CRAKE, B.A. Author of 'History of the Church under the Roman Empire,' &c. &c. Crown 8vo. 5 vols. 3s. 6d. each. Sold separately.

Edwy the Fair; or, The First Chronicle of Æscendune.

Alfgar the Dane; or, The Second Chronicle of Æscendune.

The Rival Heirs: being the Third and Last Chronicle of Æscendune.

The House of Walderne. A Tale of the Cloister and the Forest in the Days of the Barons' Wars.

Brian Fitz-Count. A Story of Wallingford Castle and Dorchester Abbey.

CRAKE.—History of the Church under the Roman Empire, A.D. 30-476. By the Rev. A. D. CRAKE, B.A. late Vicar of Cholsey, Berks. Crown 8vo. 7s. 6d.

CREIGHTON.—History of the Papacy During the Reformation. By the Rev. M. CREIGHTON, M.A. 8vo. Vols. I. and II. 1378-1464, 32s.; Vols. III. and IV. 1464-1518, 24s.

CRUMP (A.)—Works by.

A Short Enquiry into the Formation of Political Opinion, from the Reign of the Great Families to the Advent of Democracy. 8vo. 7s. 6d.

An Investigation into the Causes of the Great Fall in Prices which took place coincidently with the Demonetisation of Silver by Germany. 8vo. 6s.

CURZON.—Russia in Central Asia in 1889 and the Anglo-Russian Question. By the Hon. GEORGE N. CURZON, M.P. 8vo. 21s.

DANTE.—La Commedia di Dante. A New Text, carefully Revised with the aid of the most recent Editions and Collations. Small 8vo. 6s.

*** Fifty Copies (of which Forty-five are for Sale) have been printed on Japanese paper, £1. 1s. net.

DAVIDSON (W. L.)—Works by.

The Logic of Definition Explained and Applied. Cr. 8vo. 6s.

Leading and Important English Words Explained and Exemplified. Fcp. 8vo. 3s. 6d.

DELAND (Mrs.)—Works by.

John Ward, Preacher: a Story. Crown 8vo. 2s. boards, 2s. 6d. cloth.

Sidney: a Novel. Crown 8vo. 6s.

The Old Garden, and other Verses. Fcp. 8vo. 5s.

Florida Days. With 12 Full-page Plates (2 Etched and 4 in Colours), and about 50 Illustrations in the Text, by LOUIS K. HARLOW. 8vo. 21s.

DE LA SAUSSAYE.—A Manual of the Science of Religion. By Professor CHANTEPIE DE LA SAUSSAYE. Translated by Mrs. COLYER FERGUSSON (née MAX MÜLLER). Revised by the Author.

DE REDCLIFFE.—The Life of the Right Hon. Stratford Canning: Viscount Stratford De Redcliffe. By STANLEY LANE-POOLE. With 3 Portraits. 2 vols. 8vo. 36s.

Cabinet Edition, abridged, with 3 Portraits, 1 vol. crown 8vo. 7s. 6d.

DE SALIS (Mrs.)—Works by.

Savouries à la Mode. Fcp. 8vo. 1s. boards.

Entrées à la Mode. Fcp. 8vo. 1s. 6d. boards.

Soups and Dressed Fish à la Mode. Fcp. 8vo. 1s. 6d. boards.

Oysters à la Mode. Fcp. 8vo. 1s. 6d. boards.

Sweets and Supper Dishes à la Mode. Fcp. 8vo. 1s. 6d. boards.

Dressed Vegetables à la Mode. Fcp. 8vo. 1s. 6d. boards.

DE SALIS (Mrs.)—Works by *cont.*

Dressed **Game** and Poultry à la Mode. Fcp. 8vo. 1s. 6d. boards.

Puddings and Pastry à la Mode. Fcp. 8vo. 1s. 6d. boards.

Cakes and Confections à la Mode. Fcp. 8vo. 1s. 6d. boards.

Tempting Dishes for Small Incomes. Fcp. 8vo. 1s. 6d.

Wrinkles and Notions for every Household. Crown 8vo. 2s. 6d.

DE TOCQUEVILLE.—Democracy in America. By ALEXIS DE TOCQUEVILLE. Translated by HENRY REEVE, C.B. 2 vols. crown 8vo. 16s.

DOWELL.—A History of Taxation and Taxes in England from the Earliest Times to the Year 1885. By STEPHEN DOWELL. (4 vols. 8vo.) Vols. I. and II. The History of Taxation, 21s. Vols. III. and IV. The History of Taxes, 21s.

DOYLE (J. A.)—Works by.

The English in America: Virginia, Maryland, and the Carolinas. 8vo. 18s.

The English in America: **The** Puritan Colonies. 2 vols. 8vo. 36s.

DOYLE (A. Conan)—Works by.

Micah Clarke: his Statement as made to his three Grandchildren, Joseph, Gervas, and Reuben, during the hard Winter of 1734. With Frontispiece and Vignette. Crown 8vo. 3s. 6d.

The Captain of the Polestar; and other Tales. Crown 8vo. 6s.

Dublin University Press Series (The): a Series of Works undertaken by the Provost and Senior Fellows of Trinity College, Dublin.

Abbott's (T. K.) Codex Rescriptus Dublinensis of St. Matthew. 4to. 21s.

——— Evangeliorum Versio Antehieronymiana ex Codice Usseriano (Dublinensi). 2 vols. crown 8vo. 21s.

[Continued on next page.

Dublin University Press Series (The)—*continued*.

Allman's (C. J.) Greek Geometry from Thales to Euclid. 8vo. 10s. 6d.

Burnside (W. S.) and Panton's (A. W.) Theory of Equations. 8vo. 12s. 6d.

Casey's (John) Sequel to Euclid's Elements. Crown 8vo. 3s. 6d.

―――― Analytical Geometry of the Conic Sections. Crown 8vo. 7s. 6d.

Davies' (J. F.) Eumenides of Æschylus. With Metrical English Translation. 8vo. 7s.

Dublin Translations into Greek and Latin Verse. Edited by R. Y. Tyrrell. 8vo. 6s.

Graves' (R. P.) Life of Sir William Hamilton. 3 vols. 15s. each.

Griffin (R. W.) on Parabola, Ellipse, and Hyperbola. Crown 8vo. 6s.

Hobart's (W. K.) Medical Language of St. Luke. 8vo. 16s.

Leslie's (T. E. Cliffe) Essays in Political Economy. 8vo. 10s. 6d.

Macalister's (A.) Zoology and Morphology of Vertebrata. 8vo. 10s. 6d.

MacCullagh's (James) Mathematical and other Tracts. 8vo. 15s.

Maguire's (T.) Parmenides of Plato, Text with Introduction, Analysis, &c. 8vo. 7s. 6d.

Monck's (W. H. S.) Introduction to Logic. Crown 8vo. 5s.

Roberts' (R. A.) Examples in the Analytic 5s.

Southey's (R.) Correspondence with Caroline Bowles. Edited by E. Dowden. 8vo. 14s.

Stubbs' (J. W.) History of the University of Dublin, from its Foundation to the End of the Eighteenth Century. 8vo. 12s. 6d.

Thornhill's (W. J.) The Æneid of Virgil, freely translated into English Blank Verse. Crown 8vo. 7s. 6d.

Tyrrell's (R. Y.) Cicero's Correspondence. Vols. I, II. and III. 8vo. each 12s.

―――― The Acharnians of Aristophanes, translated into English Verse. Crown 8vo. 1s.

Webb's (T. E.) Goethe's Faust, Translation and Notes. 8vo. 12s. 6d.

―――― The Veil of Isis : a Series of Essays on Idealism. 8vo. 10s. 6d.

Wilkins' (G.) The Growth of the Homeric Poems. 8vo. 6s.

EWALD (Heinrich)—Works by.

The Antiquities of Israel. Translated from the German by H. S. SOLLY, M.A. 8vo. 12s. 6d.

The History of Israel. Translated from the German. 8 vols. 8vo. Vols. I. and II. 24s. Vols. III. and IV. 21s. Vol. V. 18s. Vol. VI. 16s. Vol. VII. 21s. Vol. VIII. with Index to the Complete Work. 18s.

FARRAR.—Language and Languages. A Revised Edition of *Chapters on Language and Families of Speech*. By F. W. FARRAR, D.D. Crown 8vo. 6s.

FIRTH.—Nation Making: a Story of New Zealand Savageism and Civilisation. By J. C. FIRTH, Author of 'Luck' and 'Our Kin across the Sea.' Crown 8vo. 6s.

FITZWYGRAM. — Horses and Stables. By Major-General Sir F. FITZWYGRAM, Bart. With 19 pages of Illustrations. 8vo. 5s.

FORD.—The Theory and Practice of Archery. By the late HORACE FORD. New Edition, thoroughly Revised and Re-written by W. BUTT, M.A. With a Preface by C. J. LONGMAN, M.A. F.S.A. 8vo. 14s.

FOX.—The Early History of Charles James Fox. By the Right Hon. Sir G. O. TREVELYAN, Bart.
Library Edition, 8vo. 18s.
Cabinet Edition, cr. 8vo. 6s.

FRANCIS.—A Book on Angling ; or, Treatise on the Art of Fishing in every branch ; including full Illustrated List of Salmon Flies. By FRANCIS FRANCIS. Post 8vo. Portrait and Plates, 15s.

FREEMAN.—The Historical Geography of Europe. By E. A. FREEMAN. With 65 Maps. 2 vols. 8vo. 31s. 6d.

FROUDE (James A.)—Works by.

The History of England, from the Fall of Wolsey to the Defeat of the Spanish Armada. 12 vols. crown 8vo. £2. 2s.

Short Studies on Great Subjects. 4 vols. crown 8vo. 24s.

FROUDE (James A.)—Works by
—*continued*.

Cæsar: a Sketch. Crown 8vo. 3s. 6d.

The English in Ireland in the Eighteenth Century. 3 vols. crown 8vo. 18s.

Oceana; or, England and Her Colonies. With 9 Illustrations. Crown 8vo. 2s. boards, 2s. 6d. cloth.

The English in the West Indies; or, the Bow of Ulysses. With 9 Illustrations. Crown 8vo. 2s. boards, 2s. 6d. cloth.

The Two Chiefs of Dunboy; an Irish Romance of the Last Century. Crown 8vo. 6s.

Thomas Carlyle, a History of his Life. 1795 to 1835. 2 vols. crown 8vo. 7s. 1834 to 1881. 2 vols. crown 8vo. 7s.

GARDINER (Samuel Rawson)—Works by.

History of England, from the Accession of James I. to the Outbreak of the Civil War, 1603-1642. 10 vols. crown 8vo. price 6s. each.

A History of the Great Civil War, 1642-1649. (3 vols.) Vol. I. 1642-1644. With 24 Maps. 8vo. 21s. Vol. II. 1644-1647. With 21 Maps. 8vo. 24s.

The Student's History of England. Illustrated under the superintendence of Mr. ST. JOHN HOPE, Secretary to the Society of Antiquaries. Vol. I. with 173 Illustrations, crown 8vo. 4s. The work will be published in Three Volumes, and also in One Volume complete.

GIBERNE—Works by.

Ralph Hardcastle's Will. By AGNES GIBERNE. With Frontispiece. Crown 8vo. 5s.

Nigel Browning. Crown 8vo. 5s.

GOETHE.—Faust. A New Translation chiefly in Blank Verse; with Introduction and Notes. By JAMES ADEY BIRDS. Crown 8vo. 6s.

Faust. The Second Part. A New Translation in Verse. By JAMES ADEY BIRDS. Crown 8vo. 6s.

GREEN.—The Works of Thomas Hill Green. Edited by R. L. NETTLESHIP (3 vols.) Vols. I. and II.—Philosophical Works. 8vo. 16s. each. Vol. III.—Miscellanies. With Index to the three Volumes and Memoir. 8vo. 21s.

The Witness of God and Faith: Two Lay Sermons. By T. H. GREEN. Fcp. 8vo. 2s.

GREVILLE.—A Journal of the Reigns of King George IV. King William IV. and Queen Victoria. By C. C. F. GREVILLE. Edited by H. REEVE. 8 vols. Cr. 8vo. 6s. en.

GREY.—Last Words to Girls. On Life in School and after School. By Mrs. WILLIAM GREY. Cr 8vo. 3s. 6d.

GWILT.—An Encyclopædia of Architecture. By JOSEPH GWILT, F.S.A. Illustrated with more than 1,700 Engravings on Wood. 8vo. 52s. 6d.

HAGGARD.—Life and its Author: an Essay in Verse. By ELLA HAGGARD. With a Memoir by H. RIDER HAGGARD, and Portrait. Fcp. 8vo. 3s. 6d.

HAGGARD (H. Rider)—Works by.

She. With 32 Illustrations by M GREIFFENHAGEN and C. H. M. KERR. Crown 8vo. 3s. 6d.

Allan Quatermain. With 31 Illustrations by C. H. M. KERR. Crown 8vo. 3s. 6d.

Maiwa's Revenge; or, the War of the Little Hand. Crown 8vo 2s. boards; 2s. 6d. cloth.

Colonel Quaritch, V.C. A Novel. Crown 8vo. 3s. 6d.

Cleopatra: being an Account of the Fall and Vengeance of Harmachis, the Royal Egyptian. With 29 Full-page Illustrations by M. Greiffenhagen and R. Caton Woodville. Crown 8vo. 6s.

Beatrice. A Novel. Cr. 8vo. 6s.

HAGGARD and LANG.—The World's Desire. By H. RIDER HAGGARD and ANDREW LANG. Crown 8vo. 6s.

HARRISON.—Myths of the Odyssey in Art and Literature. Illustrated with Outline Drawings. By JANE E. HARRISON. 8vo. 18s.

HARRISON.—The Contemporary History of the French Revolution, compiled from the 'Annual Register.' By F. BAYFORD HARRISON. Crown 8vo. 3s. 6d.

HARTE (Bret)—Works by.
In the Carquinez Woods. Fcp. 8vo. 1s. boards; 1s. 6d. cloth.
On the Frontier. 16mo. 1s.
By Shore and Sedge. 16mo. 1s.

HARTWIG (Dr.)—Works by.
The Sea and its Living Wonders. With 12 Plates and 303 Woodcuts. 8vo. 10s. 6d.
The Tropical World. With 8 Plates, and 172 Woodcuts. 8vo. 10s. 6d.
The Polar World. With 3 Maps, 8 Plates, and 85 Woodcuts. 8vo. 10s. 6d.
The Subterranean World. With 3 Maps and 80 Woodcuts. 8vo. 10s. 6d.
The Aerial World. With Map, 8 Plates, and 60 Woodcuts. 8vo. 10s. 6d.

The following books are extracted from the foregoing works by Dr. HARTWIG:—
Heroes of the Arctic Regions. With 19 Illustrations. Crown 8vo. 2s.
Wonders of the Tropical Forests. With 40 Illustrations. Crown 8vo. 2s.
Workers Under the Ground. or, Mines and Mining. With 29 Illustrations. Crown 8vo. 2s.
Marvels Over Our Heads. With 29 Illustrations. Crown 8vo. 2s.
Marvels Under Our Feet. With 22 Illustrations. Crown 8vo. 2s.
Dwellers in the Arctic Regions. With 29 Illustrations. Crown 8vo. 2s. 6d.
Winged Life in the Tropics. With 55 Illustrations. Crown 8vo. 2s. 6d.
Volcanoes and Earthquakes. With 30 Illustrations. Crown 8vo. 2s. 6d.
Wild Animals of the Tropics. With 66 Illustrations. Crown 8vo. 3s. 6d.
Sea Monsters and Sea Birds. With 75 Illustrations. Crown 8vo. 2s. 6d.
Denizens of the Deep. With 117 Illustrations. Crown 8vo. 2s. 6d.

HAVELOCK.—Memoirs of Sir Henry Havelock, K.C.B. By JOHN CLARK MARSHMAN. Cr. 8vo. 3s. 6d.

HEARN.—The Government of England; its Structure and its Development. By WILLIAM EDWARD HEARN. 8vo. 16s.

HENDERSON.—The Story of Music. By W. J. HENDERSON. Crown 8vo. 6s.

HISTORIC TOWNS. Edited by E. A. FREEMAN, D.C.L. and Rev. WILLIAM HUNT, M.A. With Maps and Plans. Crown 8vo. 3s. 6d. each.
Bristol. By Rev. W. HUNT.
Carlisle. By Rev. MANDELL CREIGHTON.
Cinque Ports. By MONTAGU BURROWS.
Colchester. By Rev. E. L. CUTTS.
Exeter. By E. A. FREEMAN.
London. By Rev. W. J. LOFTIE.
Oxford. By Rev. C. W. BOASE.
Winchester. By Rev. G. W. KITCHIN, D.D.
York. By JAMES RAINE.

HOWITT.—Visits to Remarkable Places, Old Halls, Battle-Fields, Scenes illustrative of Striking Passages in English History and Poetry. By WILLIAM HOWITT. 80 Illustrations. Cr. 8vo. 3s. 6d.

HULLAH (John)—Works by.
Course of Lectures on the History of Modern Music. 8vo. 8s. 6d.
Course of Lectures on the Transition Period of Musical History. 8vo. 10s. 6d.

HUME.—The Philosophical Works of David Hume. Edited by T. H. GREEN and T. H. GROSE. 4 vols. 8vo. 56s. Or separately, Essays, 2 vols. 28s. Treatise of Human Nature. 2 vols. 28s.

HURLBERT.—France and Her Republic: a Record of Things Seen and learned in the French Provinces during the 'Centennial Year,' 1889. By WM. HENRY HURLBERT, Author of 'Ireland under Coercion.' 1 vol. 8vo. 18s.

HUTCHINSON (Horace)—Works by.

Cricketing Saws and Stories. By HORACE HUTCHINSON. With rectilinear Illustrations by the Author. 16mo. 1s.

Some Great Golf Links. Edited by HORACE HUTCHINSON. With Illustrations.
This book is mainly a reprint of articles that have recently appeared in the *Saturday Review*.

HUTH.—The Marriage of Near Kin, considered with respect to the Law of Nations, the Result of Experience, and the Teachings of Biology. By ALFRED H. HUTH. Royal 8vo. 21s.

INGELOW (Jean)—Works by.

Poetical Works. Vols. I. and II. Fcp. 8vo. 12s. Vol. III. Fcp. 8vo. 5s.

Lyrical and Other Poems. Selected from the Writings of JEAN INGELOW. Fcp. 8vo. 2s. 6d. cloth plain; 3s. cloth gilt.

Very Young and Quite Another Story: Two Stories. Crown 8vo.

JAMES.—The Long White Mountain; or, a Journey in Manchuria, with an Account of the History, Administration, and Religion of that Province. By H. E. JAMES. With Illustrations. 8vo. 24s.

JAMESON (Mrs.)—Works by.

Legends of the Saints and Martyrs. With 19 Etchings and 187 Woodcuts. 2 vols. 8vo. 20s. *net*.

Legends of the Madonna, the Virgin Mary as represented in Sacred and Legendary Art. With 27 Etchings and 165 Woodcuts. 1 vol. 8vo. 10s. *net*.

Legends of the Monastic Orders. With 11 Etchings and 88 Woodcuts. 1 vol. 8vo. 10s. *net*.

History of Our Lord, His Types and Precursors. Completed by Lady EASTLAKE. With 31 Etchings and 281 Woodcuts. 2 vols. 8vo. 20s. *net*.

JEFFERIES.—Field and Hedgerow: last Essays of RICHARD JEFFERIES. Crown 8vo. 3s. 6d.

JENNINGS.—Ecclesia Anglicana. A History of the Church of Christ in England, from the Earliest to the Present Times. By the Rev. ARTHUR CHARLES JENNINGS, M.A. Crown 8vo. 7s. 6d.

JESSOP (G. H.)—Works by.

Judge Lynch: a Tale of the California Vineyards. Crown 8vo. 6s.

Gerald Ffrench's Friends. Cr. 8vo. 6s. A collection of Irish-American character stories.

JOHNSON.—The Patentee's Manual; a Treatise on the Law and Practice of Letters Patent. By J. JOHNSON and J. H. JOHNSON. 8vo. 10s. 6d.

JOHNSTON.—A General Dictionary of Geography, Descriptive, Physical, Statistical, and Historical; a complete Gazetteer of the World. By KEITH JOHNSTON. Medium 8vo. 42s.

JORDAN (William Leighton)—The Standard of Value. By WILLIAM LEIGHTON JORDAN. 8vo. 6s.

JUSTINIAN.—The Institutes of Justinian; Latin Text, chiefly that of Huschke, with English Introduction, Translation, Notes, and Summary. By THOMAS C. SANDARS, M.A. 8vo. 18s.

KALISCH (M. M.)—Works by.

Bible Studies. Part I. The Prophecies of Balaam. 8vo. 10s. 6d. Part II. The Book of Jonah. 8vo 10s. 6d.

Commentary on the Old Testament; with a New Translation. Vol. I. Genesis, 8vo. 18s. or adapted for the General Reader, 12s. Vol. II. Exodus, 15s. or adapted for the General Reader, 12s. Vol. III. Leviticus, Part I. 15s. or adapted for the General Reader, 8s. Vol. IV. Leviticus, Part II. 15s. or adapted for the General Reader, 8s.

Hebrew Grammar. With Exercises. Part I. 8vo. 12s. 6d Key, 5s. Part II. 12s. 6d.

KANT (Immanuel)—Works by.

Critique of Practical Reason, and other Works on the Theory of Ethics. Translated by T. K. Abbott, B.D. With Memoir. 8vo. 12s. 6d.

[Continued on next page.

KANT (Immanuel)—Works by—
continued.
Introduction to Logic, and his Essay on the Mistaken Subtilty of the Four Figures. Translated by T. K. Abbott. Notes by S. T. Coleridge. 8vo. 6s.

KENDALL (May)—Works by.
From a Garrett. Crown 8vo. 6s.
Dreams to Sell; Poems. Fcp. 8vo. 6s.
'Such is Life': a Novel. Crown 8vo. 6s.

KILLICK.— Handbook to Mill's System of Logic. By the Rev. A. H. KILLICK, M.A. Crown 8vo. 3s. 6d.

KNIGHT.—A Treasure Hunt: being the Narrative of an Expedition in the Yacht 'Alerte' to the Desert Island of Trinidada. By E. F. KNIGHT, Author of 'The Cruise of the "Falcon."' With Illustrations. Crown 8vo.

KOELLE.—Mohammed and Mohammedanism critically considered. By S. W. KOELLE, Ph.D. 8vo. 15s.

LADD.— Elements of Physiological Psychology: By GEORGE T. LADD. 8vo. 21s.

LANG (Andrew)—Works by.
Custom and Myth: Studies of Early Usage and Belief. With 15 Illustrations. Crown 8vo. 7s. 6d.
Books and Bookmen. With 2 Coloured Plates and 17 Illustrations, Cr. 8vo. 6s. 6d.
Grass of Parnassus. A Volume of Selected Verses. Fcp. 8vo. 6s.
Letters on Literature. Crown 8vo. 6s. 6d.
Old Friends: Essays in Epistolary Parody. 6s. 6d.
Ballads of Books. Edited by ANDREW LANG. Fcp. 8vo. 6s.
The Blue Fairy Book. Edited by ANDREW LANG. With numerous Illustrations by H. J. Ford and G. P. Jacomb Hood. Crown 8vo. 6s.
The Red Fairy Book. Edited by ANDREW LANG. With numerous Illustrations by H. J. Ford and Lancelot Speed. Crown 8vo. 6s.

LAVIGERIE.—Cardinal Lavigerie and the African Slave Trade. 1 vol. 8vo. 14s.

LECKY (W. E. H.)—Works by.
History of England in the Eighteenth Century. 8vo. Vols. I. & II. 1700-1760. 36s. Vols. III. & IV. 1760-1784. 36s. Vols. V. & VI. 1784-1793. 36s. Vols. VII. & VIII. 1793-1800. 36s.
The History of European Morals from Augustus to Charlemagne. 2 vols. crown 8vo. 16s.
History of the Rise and Influence of the Spirit of Rationalism in Europe. 2 vols. crown 8vo. 16s.

LEES and CLUTTERBUCK.—B. C. 1887, A Ramble in British Columbia. By J. A. LEES and W. J. CLUTTERBUCK. With Map and 75 Illustrations. Crown 8vo. 6s.

LEGER.—A History of Austro-Hungary. From the Earliest Time to the year 1889. By LOUIS LEGER. Translated from the French by Mrs. BIRKBECK HILL. With a Preface by E. A. FREEMAN, D.C.L. Crown 8vo. 10s. 6d.

LEWES.—The History of Philosophy, from Thales to Comte. By GEORGE HENRY LEWES. 2 vols. 8vo. 32s.

Light through the Crannies.—Parables and Teachings from the other Side. First Series. Cr. 8vo. 1s. swd.; 1s. 6d. cloth.

LLOYD.—The Science of Agriculture. By F. J. LLOYD. 8vo. 12s.

LONGMAN (Frederick W.)--Works by.
Chess Openings. Fcp. 8vo. 2s. 6d.
Frederick the Great and the Seven Years' War. Fcp. 8vo. 2s. 6d.

Longman's Magazine. Published Monthly. Price Sixpence.
Vols. 1-16, 8vo. price 5s. each.

Longmans' New Atlas. Political and Physical. For the Use of Schools and Private Persons. Consisting of 40 Quarto and 16 Octavo Maps and Diagrams, and 16 Plates of Views. Edited by GEO. G. CHISHOLM, M.A. B.Sc. Imp. 4to. or imp. 8vo. 12*s*. 6*d*.

LOUDON (J. C.)—Works by.

Encyclopædia of Gardening. With 1,000 Woodcuts. 8vo. 21*s*.

Encyclopædia of Agriculture; the Laying-out, Improvement, and Management of Landed Property. With 1,100 Woodcuts. 8vo. 21*s*.

Encyclopædia of Plants; the Specific Character, &c. of all Plants found in Great Britain. With 12,000 Woodcuts. 8vo. 42*s*.

LUBBOCK.—The Origin of Civilisation and the Primitive Condition of Man. By Sir J. LUBBOCK, Bart. M.P. With 5 Plates and 20 Illustrations in the text. 8vo. 18*s*.

LYALL.—The Autobiography of a Slander. By EDNA LYALL, Author of 'Donovan,' &c. Fcp. 8vo. 1*s*. sewed.

LYDE.—An Introduction to Ancient History: being a Sketch of the History of Egypt, Mesopotamia, Greece, and Rome. With a Chapter on the Development of the Roman Empire into the Powers of Modern Europe. By LIONEL W. LYDE, M.A. With 3 Coloured Maps. Crown 8vo. 3*s*.

MACAULAY (Lord).—Works of.

Complete Works of Lord Macaulay.

Library Edition, 8 vols. 8vo. £5. 5*s*.
Cabinet Edition, 16 vols. post 8vo. £4. 16*s*.

History of England from the Accession of James the Second.

Popular Edition, 2 vols. crown 8vo. 5*s*.
Student's Edition, 2 vols. crown 8vo. 12*s*.
People's Edition, 4 vols. crown 8vo. 16*s*.
Cabinet Edition, 8 vols. post 8vo. 48*s*.
Library Edition, 5 vols. 8vo. £4.

MACAULAY (Lord).—Works of.—*continued.*

Critical and Historical Essays, with Lays of Ancient Rome, in 1 volume:

Popular Edition, crown 8vo. 2*s*. 6*d*.
Authorised Edition, crown 8vo. 2*s*. 6*d*. or 3*s*. 6*d*. gilt edges.

Critical and Historical Essays:

Student's Edition, 1 vol. crown 8vo. 6*s*.
People's Edition, 2 vols. crown 8vo. 8*s*.
Trevelyan Edition, 2 vols. crown 8vo. 9*s*.
Cabinet Edition, 4 vols. post 8vo. 24*s*.
Library Edition, 3 vols. 8vo. 36*s*.

Essays which may be had separately price 6*d*. each sewed, 1*s*. each cloth:

Addison and Walpole.
Frederick the Great.
Croker's Boswell's Johnson.
Hallam's Constitutional History.
Warren Hastings. (3*d*. sewed, 6*d*. cloth.)
The Earl of Chatham (Two Essays).
Ranke and Gladstone.
Milton and Machiavelli.
Lord Bacon.
Lord Clive.
Lord Byron, and The Comic Dramatists of the Restoration.

The Essay on Warren Hastings annotated by S. HALES, 1*s*. 6*d*.

The Essay on Lord Clive annotated by H. COURTHOPE BOWEN, M.A. 2*s*. 6*d*.

Speeches:
People's Edition, crown 8vo. 3*s*. 6*d*.

Miscellaneous Writings:
People's Edition, 1 vol. crown 8vo. 4*s*. 6*d*.
Library Edition, 2 vols. 8vo. 21*s*.

Lays of Ancient Rome, &c.

Illustrated by G. Scharf, fcp. 4to. 10*s*. 6*d*.
——— Bijou Edition, 18mo. 2*s*. 6*d*. gilt top.
——— Popular Edition, fcp. 4to. 6*d*. sewed, 1*s*. cloth.
Illustrated by J. R. Weguelin, crown 8vo. 3*s*. 6*d*. cloth extra, gilt edges.
Cabinet Edition, post 8vo. 3*s*. 6*d*.
Annotated Edit. fcp. 8vo. 1*s*. sewed, 1*s*. 6*d*. cl.

[Continued on next page.

MACAULAY (Lord)—Works of—
continued.

Miscellaneous Writings and Speeches:
Popular edition, 1 vol. crown 8vo. 2s. 6d.
Student's Edition, in 1 vol. crown 8vo. 6s.
Cabinet Edition, including Indian Penal Code, Lays of Ancient Rome, and Miscellaneous Poems, 4 vols. post 8vo. 24s.

Selections from the Writings of Lord Macaulay. Edited, with Occasional Notes, by the Right Hon. Sir G. O. TREVELYAN, Bart. Crown 8vo. 6s.

The Life and Letters of Lord Macaulay. By the Right Hon. Sir G. O. TREVELYAN, Bart.
Popular Edition, 1 vol. crown 8vo. 2s. 6d.
Student's Edition, 1 vol. crown 8vo. 6s.
Cabinet Edition, 2 vols. post 8vo. 12s.
Library Edition, 2 vols. 8vo. 36s.

MACDONALD (Geo.)—Works by.

Unspoken Sermons. First and Second Series. Crown 8vo. 3s. 6d. each. Third Series. Crown 8vo. 7s. 6d.

The Miracles of Our Lord. Crown 8vo. 3s. 6d.

A Book of Strife, in the Form of the Diary of an Old Soul: Poems. 12mo. 6s.

MACFARREN—Lectures on Harmony. By Sir G. A. MACFARREN. 8vo. 12s.

MACKAIL.—Select Epigrams from the Greek Anthology. Edited, with a Revised Text, Introduction, Translation, and Notes, by J. W. MACKAIL, M.A. Fellow of Balliol College, Oxford. 8vo. 16s.

MACLEOD (Henry D.)—Works by.

The Elements of Banking. Crown 8vo. 5s.

The Theory and Practice of Banking. Vol. I. 8vo. 12s. Vol. II. 14s.

The Theory of Credit. 8vo. Vol. I. 7s. 6d.; Vol. II. Part I. 4s. 6d.

McCULLOCH—The Dictionary of Commerce and Commercial Navigation of the late J. R. MCCULLOCH. 8vo. with 11 Maps and 30 Charts, price 63s. cloth, or 70s. half-bound in russia.

MALMESBURY.—Memoirs of an Ex-Minister. By the Earl of MALMESBURY. Crown 8vo. 7s. 6d.

MANUALS OF CATHOLIC PHILOSOPHY (*Stonyhurst Series*):

Logic. By RICHARD F. CLARKE, S.J. Crown 8vo. 5s.

First Principles of Knowledge. By JOHN RICKABY, S.J. Crown 8vo. 5s.

Moral Philosophy (Ethics and Natural Law). By JOSEPH RICKABY, S.J. Crown 8vo. 5s.

General Metaphysics. By JOHN RICKABY, S.J. Crown 8vo. 5s.

Psychology. By MICHAEL MAHER, S.J. Crown 8vo. 6s. 6d.

Natural Theology. By BERNARD BOEDDER, S.J. Crown 8vo. 6s. 6d.
[*Nearly ready.*

A Manual of Political Economy. By C. S. DEVAS, Esq. M.A. Examiner in Political Economy in the Royal University of Ireland. 6s. 6d. [*In preparation.*

MARTINEAU (James)—Works by.

Hours of Thought on Sacred Things. Two Volumes of Sermons. 2 vols. crown 8vo. 7s. 6d. each.

Endeavours after the Christian Life. Discourses. Crown 8vo. 7s. 6d.

The Seat of Authority in Religion. 8vo. 14s.

MASON.—The Steps of the Sun: Daily Readings of Prose. Selected by AGNES MASON. 16mo. 3s. 6d.

MATTHEWS.—A Family Tree; and other Stories. By BRANDER MATTHEWS. Crown 8vo. 6s.

MAUNDER'S TREASURIES.

Biographical Treasury. With Supplement brought down to 1889, by Rev. JAS. WOOD. Fcp. 8vo. 6s.

Treasury of Natural History; or, Popular Dictionary of Zoology. Fcp. 8vo. with 900 Woodcuts, 6s.

Treasury of Geography, Physical, Historical, Descriptive, and Political. With 7 Maps and 16 Plates. Fcp. 8vo. 6s.

Scientific and Literary Treasury. Fcp. 8vo. 6s.

MAUNDER'S TREASURIES—*continued*.

Historical Treasury: Outlines of Universal History, Separate Histories of all Nations. Fcp. 8vo. 6*s*.

Treasury of Knowledge and Library of Reference. Comprising an English Dictionary and Grammar, Universal Gazetteer, Classical Dictionary, Chronology, Law Dictionary, &c. Fcp. 8vo. 6*s*.

The **Treasury of Bible Knowledge.** By the Rev. J. AYRE, M.A. With 5 Maps, 15 Plates, and 300 Woodcuts. Fcp. 8vo. 6*s*.

The **Treasury of Botany.** Edited by J. LINDLEY, F.R.S. and T. MOORE, F.L.S. With 274 Woodcuts and 20 Steel Plates. 2 vols. fcp. 8vo. 12*s*.

MAX MÜLLER (F.)—Works by.

Selected Essays on Language, Mythology and Religion. 2 vols. crown 8vo. 16*s*.

Lectures on the Science of Language. 2 vols. crown 8vo. 16*s*.

Three Lectures on the Science of Language and its place in General Education. Crown 8vo. 2*s*.

India, What can it Teach Us? A Course of Lectures delivered before the University of Cambridge. 8vo. 12*s*. 6*d*.

Hibbert Lectures on the Origin and Growth of Religion, as illustrated by the Religions of India. Crown 8vo. 7*s*. 6*d*.

Introduction to the Science of Religion; Four Lectures delivered at the Royal Institution. Crown 8vo. 7*s*. 6*d*.

Natural Religion. The Gifford Lectures, delivered before the University of Glasgow in 1888. Crown 8vo. 10*s*. 6*d*.

The Science of Thought. 8vo. 21*s*.

Three Introductory Lectures on the Science of Thought. 8vo. 2*s*. 6*d*.

Biographies of Words, and the Home of the Aryas. Cr 8vo. 7*s*.6*d*.

A Sanskrit Grammar for Beginners. New and Abridged Edition. By A. A. MACDONELL. Crown 8vo. 6*s*.

MAY.—**The Constitutional History of England** since the Accession of George III. 1760-1870. By the Right Hon. Sir THOMAS ERSKINE MAY, K.C.B. 3 vols. crown 8vo. 18*s*.

MEADE (L. T.)—Works by.

The O'Donnells of Inchfawn. With Frontispiece by A. CHASEMORE. Crown 8vo. 6*s*.

Daddy's Boy. With Illustrations. Crown 8vo. cloth extra, 5*s*.

Deb and the Duchess. With Illustrations by M. E. EDWARDS. Crown 8vo. cloth extra, 5*s*.

House of Surprises. With Illustrations by EDITH M. SCANNELL. Crown 8vo. cloth extra, 3*s*. 6*d*.

The Beresford Prize. With Illustrations by M. E. EDWARDS. Crown 8vo. 5*s*.

MEATH (The Earl of)—Works by.

Social Arrows: Reprinted Articles on various Social Subjects. Cr. 8vo. 5*s*.

Prosperity or Pauperism? Physical, Industrial, and Technical Training. (Edited by the EARL OF MEATH). 8vo. 5*s*.

MELBOURNE.—**The Melbourne Papers:** being a Selection from Documents in the possession of Earl Cowper, K.G. Edited by LLOYD C. SANDERS, B.A. 8vo. 18*s*.

MELVILLE (G. J. Whyte)—Novels by. Crown 8vo. 1*s*. each, boards; 1*s*. 6*d*. each, cloth.

The Gladiators.	Holmby House.
The Interpreter.	Kate Coventry.
Good for Nothing.	Digby Grand.
The Queen's Maries.	General Bounce.

MENDELSSOHN.—**The Letters of Felix Mendelssohn.** Translated by Lady WALLACE. 2 vols. cr. 8vo. 10*s*.

MERIVALE (The Very Rev. Chas.)—Works by.

History of the Romans under the Empire. Cabinet Edition, 8 vols. crown 8vo. 48*s*.

Popular Edition, 8 vols. crown 8vo. 3*s*. 6*d*. each.

[Continued on next page.

MERIVALE (The Very Rev. Chas.)—
Works by—*continued*.

The Fall of the Roman Republic:
a Short History of the Last Century of
the Commonwealth. 12mo. 7s. 6d.

General History of Rome from
B.C. 753 to A.D. 476. Cr. 8vo. 7s. 6d.

The Roman Triumvirates. With
Maps. Fcp. 8vo. 2s. 6d.

MILL.—Analysis of the Phenomena of the Human Mind.
By JAMES MILL. 2 vols. 8vo. 28s.

MILL (John Stuart)—Works by.

Principles of Political Economy.
Library Edition, 2 vols. 8vo. 30s.
People's Edition, 1 vol. crown 8vo. 5s.

A System of Logic. Cr. 8vo. 5s.

On Liberty. Crown 8vo. 1s. 4d.

On Representative Government.
Crown 8vo. 2s.

Utilitarianism. 8vo. 5s.

Examination of Sir William
Hamilton's Philosophy. 8vo. 16s.

Nature, the Utility of Religion,
and Theism. Three Essays. 8vo. 5s.

MOLESWORTH (Mrs.)—Works by.

Marrying and Giving in Marriage: a Novel. By Mrs. MOLESWORTH. Fcp. 8vo. 2s. 6d.

Silverthorns. With Illustrations by
F. NOEL PATON. Crown 8vo. 5s.

The Palace in the Garden. With
Illustrations by HARRIET M. BENNETT.
Crown 8vo. 5s.

The Third Miss St. Quentin.
Crown 8vo. 6s.

Neighbours. With Illustrations by
M. ELLEN EDWARDS. Crown 8vo. 6s.

The Story of a Spring Morning,
&c. With Illustrations by M. ELLEN
EDWARDS. Crown 8vo. 5s.

MOON (G. Washington)—Works by.
The King's English. Fcp. 8vo.
3s. 6d.

The Revisers' English. A Series
of Criticisms, showing the New Testament Revisers' Violation of the Laws of
the Language. Fcp. 8vo. 3s. 6d.

MOORE.—Dante and his Early
Biographers. By EDWARD MOORE,
D.D. Principal of St. Edmund Hall,
Oxford. Crown 8vo. 4s. 6d.

MOZLEY.—Works by.

Letters from Rome. By the
Rev. THOMAS MOZLEY, Author of 'Reminiscences of Oriel College' &c. 2 vols.
crown 8vo.

The Word. Crown 8vo. 7s. 6d.

MULHALL.— History of Prices
since the Year 1850. By MICHAEL
G. MULHALL. Crown 8vo. 6s.

MURDOCK.—The Reconstruction
of Europe: a Sketch of the Diplomatic and Military History of Continental Europe, from the Rise to the
Fall of the Second French Empire. By
HENRY MURDOCK. Crown 8vo. 9s.

MURRAY.—A Dangerous Catspaw: a Story. By DAVID CHRISTIE
MURRAY and HENRY MURRAY. Cr. 8vo.
2s. 6d.

MURRAY.—Gobi or Shamo. By
G. G. A. MURRAY. Crown 8vo. 2s.
boards; 2s. 6d. cloth.

MURRAY and HERMAN. — Wild
Darrie: a Story. By CHRISTIE MURRAY
and HENRY HERMAN. Crown 8vo. 2s.
boards; 2s. 6d. cloth.

NANSEN.—The First Crossing of
Greenland. By Dr. FRIDTJOF
NANSEN. With Maps and very numerous
Illustrations, and a Preface by J. SCOTT
KELTIE, Librarian of the Royal Geographical Society. 2 vols. 8vo. 36s.

NAPIER.—The Life of Sir Joseph
Napier, Bart. Ex-Lord Chancellor of Ireland. By ALEX.
CHARLES EWALD, F.S.A. With Portrait.
8vo. 15s.

NAPIER.—**The Lectures, Essays, and Letters of the Right Hon. Sir Joseph Napier, Bart.** late Lord Chancellor of Ireland. With an Introduction by his Daughter. Forming a Supplement to 'The Life.' With Portrait. 8vo. 12s. 6d.

NESBIT (E.)—**Works by.**

Lays and Legends. Cr. 8vo. 5s.

Leaves of Life: Verses. Cr. 8vo. 5s.

NEWMAN.—**The Letters and Correspondence of John Henry Newman** during his Life in the English Church. With a brief Autobiographical Memoir. Arranged and Edited, at Cardinal Newman's request, by Miss ANNE MOZLEY, Editor of the 'Letters of the Rev. J. B. Mozley, D.D.' With Portraits, 2 vols. 8vo.

NEWMAN (Cardinal)—**Works by.**

Apologia pro Vitâ Sua. Cabinet Edition, cr. 8vo. 6s. Cheap Edition, 3s. 6d.

The Idea of a University defined and illustrated. Crown 8vo. 7s.

Historical Sketches. 3 vols. crown 8vo. 6s. each.

The Arians of the Fourth Century. Cabinet Edition, crown 8vo. 6s. Cheap Edition, crown 8vo. 3s. 6d.

Select Treatises of St. Athanasius in Controversy with the Arians. Freely Translated. 2 vols. cr. 8vo. 15s.

Discussions and Arguments on Various Subjects. Crown 8vo. 6s.

An Essay on the Development of Christian Doctrine. Cabinet Edition, crown 8vo. 6s. Cheap Edition, crown 8vo. 3s. 6d.

Certain Difficulties felt by Anglicans in Catholic Teaching Considered. Vol. 1, crown 8vo. 7s. 6d.; Vol. 2, crown 8vo. 5s. 6d.

The Via Media of the Anglican Church, illustrated in Lectures, &c. 2 vols. crown 8vo. 6s. each.

NEWMAN (Cardinal)—Works by—*continued.*

Essays, Critical and Historical. Cabinet Edition, 2 vols. crown 8vo. 12s. Cheap Edition, 2 vols. crown 8vo. 7s.

Essays on Biblical and on Ecclesiastical Miracles. Cabinet Edition, crown 8vo. 6s. Cheap Edition, crown 8vo. 3s. 6d.

An Essay in Aid of a Grammar of Assent. Crown 8vo. 7s. 6d.

Present Position of Catholics in England. Crown 8vo. 7s. 6d.

Callista: a Tale of the Third Century. Cabinet Edition, crown 8vo. 6s. Cheap Edition, crown 8vo. 3s. 6d.

The Dream of Gerontius. 16mo. 6d. sewed, 1s. cloth.

Verses on Various Occasions. Cabinet Edition, crown 8vo. 6s. Cheap Edition, crown 8vo. 3s. 6d.

** For Cardinal Newman's other Works see Messrs. Longman's & Co.'s Catalogue of Theological Works.

NICHOLSON.—**Toxar:** a Romance. By J. SHIELD NICHOLSON, Author of 'Thoth,' &c. Crown 8vo. 6s.

NORRIS.—**Mrs. Fenton:** a Sketch. By W. E. NORRIS. Crown 8vo. 6s.

NORTHCOTT.—**Lathes and Turning,** Simple, Mechanical, and Ornamental. By W. H. NORTHCOTT. With 338 Illustrations. 8vo. 18s.

O'BRIEN.—**When we were Boys:** a Novel. By WILLIAM O'BRIEN, M.P. Cabinet Edition, crown 8vo. 6s. Cheap Edition, crown 8vo. 2s. 6d.

OLIPHANT (Mrs.)—**Novels by.**

Madam. Cr. 8vo. 1s. bds.; 1s. 6d. cl.

In Trust. Cr. 8vo. 1s. bds.; 1s. 6d. cl.

Lady Car: the Sequel of a Life. Crown 8vo. 2s. 6d.

OMAN.—**A History of Greece from the Earliest Times to the Macedonian Conquest.** By C. W. C. OMAN, M.A. F.S.A. Fellow of All Souls College, and Lecturer at New College, Oxford. With Maps and Plans. Crown 8vo. 4s. 6d.

O'REILLY (Mrs.)—Works by.

Hurstleigh Dene: a Tale. Illustrated by M. ELLEN EDWARDS. Crown 8vo. 5s.

Kirke's Mill, and other Stories. Illustrated by GORDON BROWNE. Crown 8vo. 2s. 6d.

PASTEUR.—Louis Pasteur, his Life and Labours. By his SON-IN-LAW. Translated from the French by Lady CLAUD HAMILTON. Crown 8vo. 7s. 6d.

PAYN (James)—Novels by.

The Luck of the Darrells. Cr. 8vo. 1s. boards; 1s. 6d. cloth.

Thicker than Water. Crown 8vo. 1s. boards; 1s. 6d. cloth.

PERRING (Sir PHILIP)—Works by.

Hard Knots in Shakespeare. 8vo. 7s. 6d.

The 'Works and Days' of Moses. Crown 8vo. 3s. 6d.

PHILLIPPS-WOLLEY.—Snap: a Legend of the Lone Mountain. By C. PHILLIPPS-WOLLEY, Author of 'Sport in the Crimea and Caucasus' &c. With 13 Illustrations by H. G. WILLINK. Crown 8vo. 6s.

POLE.—The Theory of the Modern Scientific Game of Whist. By W. POLE, F.R.S. Fcp. 8vo. 2s. 6d.

PORTER.—The History of the Corps of Royal Engineers. By Major-General WHITWORTH PORTER, R.E. 2 vols. 8vo. 36s.

PRENDERGAST.—Ireland, from the Restoration to the Revolution, 1660-1690. By JOHN P. PRENDERGAST. 8vo. 5s.

PRINSEP.—Virginie: a Tale of One Hundred Years Ago. By VAL PRINSEP, A.R.A. 3 vols. crown 8vo.

PROCTOR (R. A.)—Works by.

Old and New Astronomy. 12 Parts, 2s. 6d. each. Supplementary Section, 1s. Complete in 1 vol. 4to. 36s. [*In course of publication.*

PROCTOR (R. A.)—Works by—*cont.*

The Orbs Around Us; a Series of Essays on the Moon and Planets, Meteors and Comets. With Chart and Diagrams. Crown 8vo. 5s.

Other Worlds than Ours; The Plurality of Worlds Studied under the Light of Recent Scientific Researches. With 14 Illustrations. Crown 8vo. 5s.

The Moon; her Motions, Aspects, Scenery, and Physical Condition. With Plates, Charts, Woodcuts, &c. Cr. 8vo. 5s.

Universe of Stars; Presenting Researches into and New Views respecting the Constitution of the Heavens. With 22 Charts and 22 Diagrams. 8vo. 10s. 6d.

Larger Star Atlas for the Library, in 12 Circular Maps, with Introduction and 2 Index Pages. Folio, 15s. or Maps only, 12s. 6d.

The Student's Atlas. In Twelve Circular Maps on a Uniform Projection and one Scale. 8vo. 5s.

New Star Atlas for the Library, the School, and the Observatory, in 12 Circular Maps. Crown 8vo. 5s.

Light Science for Leisure Hours; Familiar Essays on Scientific Subjects. 3 vols. crown 8vo. 5s. each.

Chance and Luck; a Discussion of the Laws of Luck, Coincidences, Wagers, Lotteries, and the Fallacies of Gambling &c. Crown 8vo. 2s. boards; 2s. 6d. cloth.

Studies of Venus-Transits. With 7 Diagrams and 10 Plates. 8vo. 5s.

How to Play Whist: with the Laws and Etiquette of Whist. Crown 8vo. 3s. 6d.

Home Whist: an Easy Guide to Correct Play. 16mo 1s.

The Stars in their Seasons. An Easy Guide to a Knowledge of the Star Groups, in 12 Maps. Roy. 8vo. 5s.

Star Primer. Showing the Starry Sky Week by Week, in 24 Hourly Maps. Crown 4to. 2s. 6d.

The Seasons Pictured in 48 Sun-Views of the Earth, and 24 Zodiacal Maps, &c. Demy 4to. 5s.

Strength and Happiness. With 9 Illustrations. Crown 8vo. 5s.

PROCTOR (R. A.)—Works by—*cont.*

Strength: How to get Strong and keep Strong, with Chapters on Rowing and Swimming, Fat, Age, and the Waist. With 9 Illustrations. Crown 8vo. 2s.

Rough Ways Made Smooth. Familiar Essays on Scientific Subjects. Crown 8vo. 5s.

Our Place Among Infinities. A Series of Essays contrasting our Little Abode in Space and Time with the Infinities Around us. Crown 8vo. 5s.

The Expanse of Heaven. Essays on the Wonders of the Firmament. Crown 8vo. 5s.

The Great Pyramid, Observatory, Tomb, and Temple. With Illustrations. Crown 8vo. 5s.

Pleasant Ways in Science. Crown 8vo. 5s.

Myths and Marvels of Astronomy. Crown 8vo. 5s.

Nature Studies. By Grant Allen, A. Wilson, T. Foster, E. Clodd, and R. A. Proctor. Crown 8vo. 5s.

Leisure Readings. By E. Clodd, A. Wilson, T. Foster, A. C. Ranyard, and R. A. Proctor. Crown 8vo. 5s.

PROTHERO.—The Pioneers and Progress of English Farming. By Rowland E. Prothero. Cr. 8vo. 5s.

PRYCE.—**The Ancient British Church**: an Historical Essay. By John Pryce, M.A. Crown 8vo. 6s.

RANSOME.—**The Rise of Constitutional Government in England**: being a Series of Twenty Lectures on the History of the English Constitution delivered to a Popular Audience. By Cyril Ransome, M.A. Crown 8vo. 6s.

RAWLINSON.—The History of Phœnicia. By George Rawlinson, M.A. Canon of Canterbury, &c. With numerous Illustrations. 8vo. 24s.

READER (Emily E.)—Works by. **Echoes of Thought**: a Medley of Verse. Fcp. 8vo. 5s. cloth, gilt top.

READER (Emily E.)—Works by—*continued.*

The Ghost of Brankinshaw and other Tales. With 9 Illustrations. Fcp. 8vo. 2s. 6d. cloth extra, gilt edges.

Voices from Flower-Land, in Original Couplets. A Birthday-Book and Language of Flowers. 16mo. 1s. 6d. limp cloth; 2s. 6d. roan, gilt edges, or in vegetable vellum, gilt top.

Fairy Prince Follow-my-Lead; or, the Magic Bracelet. Crown 8vo. 2s. 6d. gilt edges; or 3s. 6d. vegetable vellum, gilt edges.

RENDLE and NORMAN.—The Inns of Old Southwark, and their Associations. By William Rendle, F.R.C.S. and Philip Norman, F.S.A. With numerous Illustrations. Roy. 8vo. 28s.

RIBOT.—**The Psychology of Attention.** By Th. Ribot. Crown 8vo. 3s.

RICH.—A Dictionary of Roman and Greek Antiquities. With 2,000 Woodcuts. By A. Rich. Cr. 8vo. 7s. 6d.

RICHARDSON.—National Health. Abridged from 'The Health of Nations.' A Review of the Works of Sir Edwin Chadwick, K.C.B. By Dr. B. W. Richardson. Crown, 4s. 6d.

RILEY.—**Athos;** or, the Mountain of the Monks. By Athelstan Riley, M.A. F.R.G.S. With Map and 29 Illustrations. 8vo. 21s.

RIVERS (Thomas)—Works by.

The Orchard-House. With 25 Woodcuts. Crown 8vo. 5s.

The Miniature Fruit Garden; or, the Culture of Pyramidal and Bush Fruit Trees. With 32 Illustrations. Fcp. 8vo. 4s.

ROBERTS.—**Greek** the Language of Christ and His Apostles. By Alexander Roberts, D.D. 8vo. 18s.

ROGET.—**Thesaurus of English Words and Phrases.** Classified and Arranged so as to facilitate the Expression of Ideas. By Peter M. Roget. Crown 8vo. 10s. 6d.

RONALDS.—The Fly-Fisher's Entomology. By ALFRED RONALDS. With 20 Coloured Plates. 8vo. 14s.

ROSSETTI.—A Shadow of Dante: being an Essay towards studying Himself, his World, and his Pilgrimage. By MARIA FRANCESCA ROSSETTI. With Illustrations. Crown 8vo. 10s. 6d.

RUSSELL.—A Life of Lord John Russell (Earl Russell, K.G.). By SPENCER WALPOLE. With 2 Portraits. 2 vols. 8vo. 36s.

SCHELLEN.—Spectrum Analysis in its Application to Terrestrial Substances, and the Physical Constitution of the Heavenly Bodies. By Dr. H. SCHELLEN. With 14 Plates and 291 Woodcuts. 8vo. 31s. 6d.

SCOTT.—Weather Charts and Storm Warnings. By R. H. SCOTT, F.R.S. With Illustrations. Cr. 8vo. 6s.

SEEBOHM (Frederick)—Works by.

The Oxford Reformers—John Colet, Erasmus, and Thomas More; a History of their Fellow-Work. 8vo. 14s.

The Era of the Protestant Revolution. With Map. Fcp. 8vo. 2s. 6d.

The English Village Community Examined in its Relations to the Manorial and Tribal Systems, &c, 13 Maps and Plates. 8vo. 16s.

SEWELL.—Stories and Tales. By ELIZABETH M. SEWELL. Crown 8vo. 1s. 6d. each, cloth plain; 2s. 6d. each, cloth extra, gilt edges:—

Amy Herbert.
The Earl's Daughter.
The Experience of Life.
A Glimpse of the World.
Cleve Hall.
Katharine Ashton.
Margaret Percival.
Laneton Parsonage.
Ursula.
Gertrude.
Ivors.

SHAKESPEARE.—Bowdler's Family Shakespeare. 1 vol. 8vo. With 36 Woodcuts, 14s. or in 6 vols. fcp. 8vo. 21s.

Outlines of the Life of Shakespeare. By J. O. HALLIWELL-PHILLIPPS. 2 vols. Royal 8vo. £1. 1s.

SHAKESPEARE.—The Shakespeare Birthday Book. By MARY F. DUNBAR. 32mo. 1s. 6d. cloth. With Photographs, 32mo. 5s. Drawing-Room Edition, with Photographs, fcp. 8vo. 10s. 6d.

Shakespeare's True Life. By JAMES WALTER. With 500 Illustrations. Imp. 8vo. 21s.

SHORT.—Sketch of the History of the Church of England to the Revolution of 1688. By T. V. SHORT, D.D. Crown 8vo. 7s. 6d.

SILVER LIBRARY, THE. Crown 8vo. 3s. 6d. each volume.

She: a History of Adventure. By H. RIDER HAGGARD. With 32 Illustrations. 3s. 6d.

Allan Quatermain. By H. RIDER HAGGARD. With 20 Illustrations. 3s. 6d.

Colonel Quaritch, V.C.: a Tale of Country Life. By H. RIDER HAGGARD. With Frontispiece and Vignette. 3s. 6d.

Micah Clarke: His Statement. A Tale of Monmouth's Rebellion. By A. CONAN DOYLE. With Frontispiece and Vignette. 3s. 6d.

Petland Revisited. By the Rev. J. G. WOOD. With 33 Illustrations. 3s. 6d.

Strange Dwellings: a Description of the Habitations of Animals. By the Rev. J. G. WOOD. With 60 Illustrations. 3s. 6d.

Out of Doors. Original Articles on Practical Natural History. By the Rev. J. G. WOOD. With 11 Illustrations. 3s. 6d.

Familiar History of Birds. By the late EDWARD STANLEY, D.D. Lord Bishop of Norwich. With 160 Woodcuts. 3s. 6d.

Eight Years in Ceylon. By Sir S. W. BAKER. With 6 Illustrations. 3s. 6d.

Rifle and Hound in Ceylon. By Sir S. W. BAKER. With 6 Illustrations. 3s. 6d.

Memoirs of Major-General Sir Henry Havelock. By JOHN CLARK MARSHMAN. With Portrait. 3s. 6d.

SILVER LIBRARY, THE—*continued.*

Visits to Remarkable Places, Old Halls, Battlefields, Scenes Illustrative of Striking Passages in English History and Poetry. By WILLIAM HOWITT. With 80 Illustrations. 3*s.* 6*d.*

Field and Hedgerow. Last Essays of RICHARD JEFFERIES. With Portrait. 3*s.* 6*d.*

Story of Creation: a Plain account of Evolution. By EDWARD CLODD. With 77 Illustrations. 3*s.* 6*d.*

Life of the Duke of Wellington. By the Rev. G. R. GLEIG, M.A. With Portrait. 3*s.* 6*d.*

History of the Romans under the Empire. By the Very Rev. CHARLES MERIVALE, D.C.L. Dean of Ely. 8 vols. Each 3*s.* 6*d.*

Cæsar: a Sketch. By JAMES A. FROUDE. 3*s.* 6*d.*

Thomas Carlyle: a History of his Life. By J. A. FROUDE, M.A. 1795-1835, 2 vols. 7*s.* 1834-1881, 2 vols. 7*s.*

Apologia pro Vitâ Suâ. By Cardinal NEWMAN. 3*s.* 6*d.*

Callista: a Tale of the Third Century. By Cardinal NEWMAN. 3*s.* 6*d.*

Essays, Critical and Historical. By Cardinal NEWMAN. 2 vols. crown 8vo. 7*s.*

An Essay on the Development of Christian Doctrine. By Cardinal NEWMAN. Crown 8vo. 3*s.* 6*d.*

The Arians of the Fourth Century. By CARDINAL NEWMAN. 3*s.* 6*d.*

Verses on Various Occasions. By CARDINAL NEWMAN. 3*s.* 6*d.*

Two Essays on Biblical and Ecclesiastical Miracles. By CARDINAL NEWMAN. 3*s.* 6*d.*

SMITH (Gregory).—Fra Angelico, and other Short Poems. By GREGORY SMITH. Crown 8vo. 4*s.* 6*d.*

SMITH (J. H.)—The White Umbrella in Mexico. By J. HOPKINSON SMITH. Fcp. 8vo. 6*s.* 6*d.*

SMITH (R. Bosworth).—Carthage and the Carthagenians. By R. BOSWORTH SMITH, M.A. Maps, Plans, &c. Crown 8vo. 6*s.*

Sophocles. Translated into English Verse. By ROBERT WHITELAW, M.A. Assistant-Master in Rugby School; late Fellow of Trinity College, Cambridge. Crown 8vo. 8*s.* 6*d.*

SOUTHEY.—The Poetical Works of Robert Southey. With Portrait. Royal 8vo. 14*s.*

STANLEY.—A Familiar History of Birds. By E. STANLEY, D.D. With 160 Woodcuts. Crown 8vo. 3*s.* 6*d.*

STEEL (J. H.)—Works by.

A Treatise on the Diseases of the Dog; being a Manual of Canine Pathology. Especially adapted for the Use of Veterinary Practitioners and Students. 88 Illustrations. 8vo. 10*s.* 6*d.*

A Treatise on the Diseases of the Ox; being a Manual of Bovine Pathology specially adapted for the use of Veterinary Practitioners and Students. 2 Plates and 117 Woodcuts. 8vo. 15*s.*

A Treatise on the Diseases of the Sheep: being a Manual of Ovine Pathology. Especially adapted for the use of Veterinary Practitioners and Students. With Coloured Plate and 99 Woodcuts. 8vo. 12*s.*

STEPHEN.—Essays in Ecclesiastical Biography. By the Right Hon. Sir J. STEPHEN. Cr. 8vo. 7*s.* 6*d.*

STEPHENS.—A History of the French Revolution. By H. MORSE STEPHENS, Balliol College, Oxford. 3 vols. 8vo. Vol. I. 18*s. Ready.* Vol. II. *in the Press.*

STEVENSON (Robt. Louis)—Works by.

A Child's Garden of Verses. Small fcp. 8vo. 5*s.*

The Dynamiter. Fcp. 8vo. 1*s.* swd. 1*s.* 6*d.* cloth.

Strange Case of Dr. Jekyll and Mr. Hyde. Fcp. 8vo. 1*s.* swd.; 1*s.* 6*d.* cloth.

STEVENSON and OSBOURNE.—**The Wrong Box.** By ROBERT LOUIS STEVENSON and LLOYD OSBOURNE. Crown 8vo. 5s.

STOCK.—Deductive **Logic.** By ST. GEORGE STOCK. Fcp. 8vo. 3s. 6d.

'STONEHENGE.'—**The Dog in** Health and **Disease.** By 'STONEHENGE.' With 84 Wood Engravings. Square crown 8vo. 7s. 6d.

STRONG and LOGEMAN.—Introduction to the Study of the History of Language. By HERBERT A. STRONG, M.A. LL.D. Professor of Latin, University College, Liverpool; and WILLIAM S. LOGEMAN, Newton School, Rockferry, Birkenhead. 8vo.

SULLY (James)—Works by.

Outlines of Psychology, with Special Reference to the Theory of Education. 8vo. 12s. 6d.

The Teacher's Handbook of Psychology, on the Basis of 'Outlines of Psychology.' Cr. 8vo. 6s. 6d.

Supernatural Religion; an Inquiry into the Reality of Divine Revelation. 3 vols. 8vo. 36s.

Reply (A) to Dr. Lightfoot's **Essays.** By the Author of 'Supernatural Religion.' 1 vol. 8vo. 6s.

SWINBURNE.—**Picture** Logic; an Attempt to Popularise the Science of Reasoning. By A. J. SWINBURNE, B.A. Post 8vo. 5s.

SYMES.—Prelude to Modern History: being a Brief Sketch of the World's History from the Third to the Ninth Century. By J. E. SYMES, M.A. University College, Nottingham. With 5 Maps. Crown 8vo. 2s. 6d.

TAYLOR.—A Student's Manual of the History of India, from the Earliest Period to the Present Time. By Colonel MEADOWS TAYLOR, C.S.I &c. Crown 8vo. 7s. 6d.

THOMPSON (D. Greenleaf)—**Works** by.

The Problem of Evil: an Introduction to the Practical Sciences. 8vo. 10s. 6d.

THOMPSON (D. Greenleaf)—**Works** by—*continued*.

A System of Psychology. 2 vols. 8vo. 36s.

The Religious Sentiments of the Human Mind. 8vo. 7s. 6d.

Social Progress: an Essay. 8vo. 7s. 6d.

Three in Norway. By Two of THEM. With a Map and 59 Illustrations. Cr. 8vo. 2s. boards; 2s. 6d. cloth.

Times and Days: being Essays in Romance and History. Fcp. 8vo. 5s.

TOMSON.—**The Bird Bride:** a Volume of Ballads and Sonnets. By GRAHAM R. TOMSON. Fcp. 8vo. 6s.

TOYNBEE.—Lectures on the Industrial Revolution of the 18th Century in England. By the late ARNOLD TOYNBEE, Tutor of Balliol College, Oxford. Together with a Short Memoir by B. JOWETT, Master of Balliol College, Oxford. 8vo. 10s. 6d.

TREVELYAN (Sir G. O. Bart.)—**Works** by.

The Life and **Letters of Lord** Macaulay.
POPULAR EDITION, 1 vol. cr. 8vo. 2s. 6d.
STUDENT'S EDITION, 1 vol. cr. 8vo. 6s.
CABINET EDITION, 2 vols. cr. 8vo. 12s.
LIBRARY EDITION, 2 vols. 8vo. 36s.

The Early History of Charles James Fox. Library Edition, 8vo. 18s. Cabinet Edition, crown 8vo. 6s.

TROLLOPE (Anthony).—**Novels by.**

The Warden. Crown 8vo. 1s. boards; 1s. 6d. cloth.

Barchester Towers. Crown 8vo. 1s. boards; 1s. 6d. cloth.

VIGNOLES.—The Life of C. B. Vignoles, F.R.S. Soldier and Civil Engineer. By his Son, OLINTHUS J. VIGNOLES, M.A. 8vo. 16s.

VILLE.—**On Artificial Manures,** their Chemical Selection and Scientific Application to Agriculture. By GEORGES VILLE. Translated and edited by W. CROOKES. With 31 Plates. 8vo. 21*s.*

VIRGIL.—**Publi Vergili Maronis Bucolica, Georgica, Æneis**; the Works of VIRGIL, Latin Text, with English Commentary and Index. By B. H. KENNEDY, D.D. Cr. 8vo. 10*s.* 6*d.*

The **Æneid of Virgil**. Translated into English Verse. By JOHN CONINGTON, M.A. Crown 8vo. 6*s.*

The **Poems of Virgil**. Translated into English Prose. By JOHN CONINGTON, M.A. Crown 8vo. 6*s.*

The **Eclogues and Georgics of Virgil.** Translated from the Latin by J. W. MACKAIL, M.A. Fellow of Balliol College, Oxford. Printed on Dutch Hand-made Paper. Royal 16mo. 5*s.*

WAKEMAN and HASSALL.—**Essays Introductory to the Study of English Constitutional History.** By Resident Members of the University of Oxford. Edited by HENRY OFFLEY WAKEMAN, M.A. Fellow of All Souls College, and ARTHUR HASSALL, M.A. Student of Christ Church. Crown 8vo. 6*s.*

WALKER.—**The Correct Card**; or, How to Play at Whist; a Whist Catechism. By Major A. CAMPBELL-WALKER, F.R.G.S. Fcp. 8vo. 2*s.* 6*d.*

WALPOLE.—**History of England from the Conclusion of the Great War in 1815 to 1858.** By SPENCER WALPOLE. Library Edition. 5 vols. 8vo. £4. 10*s.* Cabinet Edition. 6 vols. crown 8vo. 6*s.* each.

WELLINGTON.—**Life of the Duke of Wellington.** By the Rev. G. R. GLEIG, M.A. Crown 8vo. 3*s.* 6*d.*

WELLS.—**Recent Economic Changes** and their Effect on the Production and Distribution of Wealth and the Well-being of Society. By DAVID A. WELLS, LL.D. D.C.L. late United States Special Commissioner of Revenue, &c. Crown 8vo. 10*s.* 6*d.*

WENDT —**Papers on Maritime Legislation,** with a Translation of the German Mercantile Laws relating to Maritime Commerce. By ERNEST EMIL WENDT, D.C.L. Royal 8vo. £1. 11*s.* 6*d.*

WEST.—**Lectures on the Diseases of Infancy and Childhood.** By CHARLES WEST, M.D. 8vo. 18*s.*

WEYMAN.—**The House of the Wolf:** a Romance. By STANLEY J. WEYMAN. Crown 8vo. 6*s.*

WHATELY (E. Jane)—**Works by.**

English **Synonyms**. Edited by R. WHATELY, D.D. Fcp. 8vo. 3*s.*

Life and Correspondence of Richard Whately, D.D. late Archbishop of Dublin. With Portrait. Crown 8vo. 10*s.* 6*d.*

WHATELY (Archbishop)—**Works by.**

Elements of Logic. Cr. 8vo. 4*s.* 6*d.*

Elements of Rhetoric. Crown 8vo. 4*s.* 6*d.*

Lessons on Reasoning. Fcp. 8vo. 1*s.* 6*d.*

Bacon's **Essays**, with Annotations. 8vo. 10*s.* 6*d.*

WILCOCKS.—**The Sea Fisherman.** Comprising the Chief Methods of Hook and Line Fishing in the British and other Seas, and Remarks on Nets, Boats, and Boating. By J. C. WILCOCKS. Profusely Illustrated. Crown 8vo. 6*s.*

WILLICH.—**Popular Tables for** giving Information for ascertaining the value of Lifehold, Leasehold, and Church Property, the Public Funds, &c. By CHARLES M. WILLICH. Edited by H. BENCE JONES. Crown 8vo. 10*s.* 6*d.*

WILLOUGHBY.—**East Africa and its Big Game.** The Narrative of a Sporting Trip from Zanzibar to the Borders of the Masai. By Capt. Sir JOHN C. WILLOUGHBY, Bart. Illustrated by G. D. Giles and Mrs. Gordon Hake. Royal 8vo. 21*s.*

WITT (Prof.)—**Works by.** Translated by FRANCES YOUNGHUSBAND.

The Trojan War. Crown 8vo. 2s.

Myths of Hellas; or, Greek Tales. Crown 8vo. 3s. 6d.

The Wanderings of Ulysses. Crown 8vo. 3s.

The Retreat of the Ten Thousand; being the Story of Xenophon's 'Anabasis.' With Illustrations.

WOLFF.—**Rambles in the Black Forest.** By HENRY W. WOLFF. Crown 8vo. 7s. 6d.

WOOD (Rev. J. G.)—**Works by.**

Homes Without Hands; a Description of the Habitations of Animals, classed according to the Principle of Construction. With 140 Illustrations. 8vo. 10s. 6d.

Insects at Home; a Popular Account of British Insects, their Structure, Habits, and Transformations. With 700 Illustrations. 8vo. 10s. 6d.

Insects Abroad; a Popular Account of Foreign Insects, their Structure, Habits, and Transformations. With 600 Illustrations. 8vo. 10s. 6d.

Bible Animals; a Description of every Living Creature mentioned in the Scriptures. With 112 Illustrations. 8vo. 10s. 6d.

Strange Dwellings; a Description of the Habitations of Animals, abridged from 'Homes without Hands.' With 60 Illustrations. Crown 8vo. 3s. 6d.

Out of Doors; a Selection of Original Articles on Practical Natural History. With 11 Illustrations. Crown 8vo. 3s. 6d.

Petland Revisited. With 33 Illustrations. Crown 8vo. 3s. 6d.

The following books are extracted from the foregoing works by the Rev. J. G. WOOD:

Social Habitations and Parasitic Nests. With 18 Illustrations. Crown 8vo. 2s.

The Branch Builders. With 28 Illustrations. Crown 8vo. 2s. 6d.

Wild Animals of the Bible. With 29 Illustrations. Crown 8vo. 3s. 6d.

WOOD (Rev. J. G.)—**Works by**—*cont.*

Domestic Animals of the Bible. With 23 Illustrations. Crown 8vo. 3s. 6d.

Bird-Life of the Bible. With 32 Illustrations. Crown 8vo. 3s. 6d.

Wonderful Nests. With 30 Illustrations. Crown 8vo. 3s. 6d.

Homes under the Ground. With 28 Illustrations. Crown 8vo. 3s. 6d.

YOUATT (William)—**Works by.**

The Horse. Revised and enlarged. 8vo. Woodcuts, 7s. 6d.

The Dog. Revised and enlarged. 8vo. Woodcuts, 6s.

YOUNGHUSBAND (Frances)—**Works by.**

The Story of our Lord, told in Simple Language for Children. With 25 Illustrations on Wood from Pictures by the Old Masters. Crown 8vo. 2s. 6d.

The Story of Genesis. Crown 8vo. 2s. 6d.

ZELLER (Dr. E.)—**Works by.**

History of Eclecticism in Greek Philosophy. Translated by SARAH F. ALLEYNE. Crown 8vo. 10s. 6d.

The Stoics, Epicureans, and Sceptics. Translated by the Rev. O. J. REICHEL, M.A. Crown 8vo. 15s.

Socrates and the Socratic Schools. Translated by the Rev. O. J. REICHEL, M.A. Crown 8vo. 10s. 6d.

Plato and the Older Academy. Translated by SARAH F. ALLEYNE and ALFRED GOODWIN, B.A. Crown 8vo. 18s.

The Pre-Socratic Schools: a History of Greek Philosophy from the Earliest Period to the time of Socrates. Translated by SARAH F. ALLEYNE. 2 vols. crown 8vo. 30s.

Outlines of the History of Greek Philosophy. Translated by SARAH F. ALLEYNE and EVELYN ABBOTT. Crown 8vo. 10s. 6d.

Spottiswoode & Co. Printers, New-street Square, London.

www.ingramcontent.com/pod-product-compliance
Lightning Source LLC
Chambersburg PA
CBHW020151170426
43199CB00010B/991